All Scripture references taken from the KJV of the Holy Bible, unless otherwise indicated.

BLOCKERS. ***How To Recognize, Move Them, or Navigate Around Them***

by Dr. Marlene Miles

Freshwater Press 2026

Freshwaterpress9@gmail.com

ISBN: 978-1-971933-71-9

I0835103

Paperback Version

Table of Contents

BLOCKERS.

BLOCKERS.

I used to work with an older woman who called everybody a blocker. Every week she had a new warning for the younger women in the building. “That man is a blocker.” “Girl, don’t waste your time. He’s a blocker.” “That one right there will delay your whole life.”

At the time, I laughed it off, but years later, I realized something uncomfortable, she wasn’t wrong. Not about every man, of course. Not every difficult relationship is sabotage. Not every delay is spiritual warfare. Not every inconvenience is an enemy assignment.

But blockers are real.

Most people have experienced them even if they never had language for them.

Why does everything sometimes feel harder than it should? Why do certain seasons feel like constant interruption? Why do some people repeatedly approach movement only to get tangled in confusion, exhaustion, delay, distraction, bad timing, emotional chaos, draining relationships, or opportunities that collapse at the last minute?

Blockers.

Many people spend years trying to move forward while something consistently stands in the way.

Sometimes the blocker is obvious: fear, addiction, debt, insecurity, manipulation, toxic relationships, destructive habits. But other blockers are subtle. Distraction. Emotional exhaustion. False urgency. Misplaced loyalty. Chronic confusion. Performance culture. Emotionally expensive people. Environments that quietly consume momentum.

Some blockers even arrive disguised as blessings. They enter through attraction, attention, opportunity, flattery, romance, guilt, obligation, "potential," or the desire to help and save, but they are people who slowly consume years of your life in return. That is what makes blockers dangerous: many people do not recognize them until enormous amounts of time, Peace, energy, opportunity, clarity, and movement have already been consumed.

Blockers are more than ordinary obstacles.

Obstacles are inert. They simply exist. A mountain is an obstacle. A fallen tree is an obstacle. A mountain is an obstacle. A locked gate is an obstacle, but blockers are different. Blockers interfere. Disrupt timing. Create confusion. Stagnate movement.

Some blockers are people. Some are systems. Some are environments. Some are emotional. Some are spiritual. Some are inherited. Some are internal.

Some are standing so close to your life that you no longer recognize them as blockers at all.

Obstacles do not think; they just sit there. They do not strategize. They do not react to your movement. They simply sit where they are.

Blockers are different.

A blocker is active. A blocker responds to movement. A blocker interferes. A blocker recognizes progress and inserts itself into pathways, relationships, systems, timing, opportunities, clarity, Peace, or momentum in order to hinder advancement. Blockers delay. They stagnate. They consume energy. They redirect attention. They obstruct movement. Some are internalized. Some are visible. Some are disguised. Some are inherited. Some are self-created. Some are accidental. Some are strategic.

Most people understand obstacles. Far fewer understand blockers.

An obstacle can be inconvenient without being personal. Victims of blockers often feel targeted because blockers interact with movement itself. Many people begin noticing blockers during periods of transition, advancement, healing, clarity, growth, or preparation. Suddenly, confusion increases. Delays increase. Interruptions multiply. Emotional chaos appears. Strange resistance emerges around otherwise simple movement. Relationships shift. Draining people reappear. Distractions intensify. Fatigue increases. Focus breaks apart. Things that should move smoothly become unusually difficult.

This does not mean every inconvenience is warfare. It does not mean every difficult person is an enemy. It does not mean every delay is sabotage. Wisdom requires balance. A flat tire is sometimes just a flat tire. A missed opportunity is sometimes poor timing. A closed door may actually be protection. Not every hard season is an attack. But many people spend years of their lives failing to recognize consistent patterns of obstruction because they have never learned the difference between ordinary obstacles and active blockers.

Blockers often reveal themselves through repetition. The same type of disruption appears over and over again. The same emotional cycle repeats. The same kind of relationship drains movement. The same confusion arises whenever progress begins. The same instability interrupts Peace. The same patterns emerge around money, clarity, opportunity, or purpose. At some point, wisdom must ask a serious question: Is this random, or is something consistently interfering with movement?

Some blockers are obvious. A controlling person can become a blocker. An abusive system can become a blocker. Fear, addiction, and chronic distraction can become blockers. Emotional dependency, pride, sin – so many things can become blockers. A person's own mindset can become a blocker. A nation or a government, an unhealthy family structure, a manipulative relationship—all these can become blockers.

Some blockers are external, but some are deeply internal.

Other blockers are far more subtle because they arrive disguised as opportunity, affection, help, comfort, attention, romance, networking, loyalty, or obligation. Some blockers are attractive. Some blockers are flattering. Some blockers make people feel chosen, desired, important, needed, admired, or emotionally secure. These are often the most dangerous blockers because people protect what comforts them even when it is quietly obstructing their future.

There are also seasons in life where the blocker is not a person at all, but positioning. Timing itself can function as a blocker. A person can attempt movement before maturity, before preparation, before clarity, or before the proper season has arrived. In those moments, what feels like obstruction may actually be restraint. Not every blocker is evil. Some blockers protect people from self-destruction. Some barriers exist because a person is not yet ready for what they are demanding access to.

The goal of this book is to develop awareness. A person who understands blockers begins to move differently. They become more observant. More discerning. More strategic. More peaceful. More intentional about relationships, environments, timing, access, and agreement.

Movement matters in life. Access matters. Timing matters. Clarity matters. Peace matters. Many people remain trapped for years not because they lack talent, intelligence, beauty, ability, opportunity, or desire, but because they never properly identified what was consistently standing in the way.

Before a blocker can be moved, defeated, navigated around, outlasted, or overcome, it must first be recognized for what it is.

Blockers are bigger than obstacles. When things stop movement or interrupt flow they may be a blocker. Things preventing access, things delaying destiny, bottlenecking progress, or standing in gates, doors, pathways, momentum--, those are blockers.

It's not about you not getting your way all the time and then assigning the term blocker to everything.

Not every blocker is demonic.

Some blockers are structural. Some are consequences. Some are Wisdom, some are timing. But some blockers truly are assignments. The problem is not that blockers exist, the problem is failing to recognize them before they consume years of your life.

To block, as a verb means to enclose or shut up, so as to hinder egress or passage. It means to stop up, to obstruct, by placing obstacles in the way, as, to *block* up a town, or a road.

THE BLOCK

In falconry, the perch whereon a bird of prey is kept is called a block. This powerful, dangerous creature sits there until it is time to hunt. The bird is not broken. The bird is not caged. Its wings still work. Its eyesight is still sharp. Its talons are still lethal. It still possesses the instincts of a hunter. It is visibly magnificent, but it is still a bird of prey.

In falconry, the perch is where the bird of prey is kept between flights. It is the place of waiting, observation, conditioning, and controlled release. The bird is elevated enough to see, but restrained enough not to fully move. That alone is profound, because many people think limitation always appears as obvious ruin. Sometimes limitation appears as partial freedom. Sometimes the enemy does not need to destroy a person if he can put the block in their path. If this blocker is especially evil or connected there may be unseen things on the block that will layer the stalling or hindrance of that man.

The unseen bird on the perch becomes both predator and evil watchman. It sees everything. Nothing escapes its sight. It watches movement below. It tracks activity in the environment. It is alert, discerning, aware.

If someone or something is stopped by the block, itself an obstacle, then a predatory animal perched there would have easy prey.

There are people whose spiritual gifts still function while their movement has been restricted. Their vision still works. Their instincts still work. Their spiritual sensitivity still works. They still carry power, intelligence, creativity, insight, and authority. But something has conditioned them into staying within a controlled radius by the blocks that have been erected. If they are visible, they are visible. If they are unseen, they are in the spirit.

That is what makes blocker systems so subtle. Sometimes the goal is not destruction. Sometimes the goal is supervised existence. A person remains functional but contained. They may remain strong but redirected. Gifted but positioned. Powerful but interrupted. They experience enough movement to believe they are free while never fully entering the altitude, territory, or momentum they were created for. They don't even know they are the victim of a blocker.

The point is, there is a block, or a blockade. Simpler but like in war the enemy is approaching head on, but there is a battalion sneaking up the rear to surround and overtake. That warfare pattern appears repeatedly in Scripture; there is visible opposition and hidden, unseen positioning happening simultaneously.

One example is when enemies attempted to surround Israel through coordinated positioning rather than direct frontal attack alone. Ambushes, flanking movements, and surrounding armies appear throughout the Old Testament military narratives.

A particularly strong example is found in 2 Chronicles 20, where multiple enemy groups formed an alliance against Judah. The threat was not merely one enemy approaching directly. It was coordinated encirclement pressure. Jehoshaphat's fear came partly from realizing the scale and positioning of the opposition.

Another important pattern is Ai in Joshua, where ambush strategy was used. Part of the force drew attention in one direction while another positioned itself elsewhere. Scripture repeatedly shows warfare involving ambushes and siege tactics as well as other arts of war.

Don't only focus on the obvious blocker directly in front of you, failing to notice what's all around. There are things in the spirit that you can't even see. On the cover of this book there is a big cement block, but sitting there is a pretty girl, do you see her as part of the blockade, or is she just a pretty girl? There is a falcon and the block is his perch. He is a trained predator so why is he sitting there?

So don't get too busy fighting one visible issue, while other things are developing or already present around the perimeter of your life.

That's the "siege" dynamic. Sometimes the visible battle is not the whole battle. While your attention is fixed on one enemy in front of you, other pressures may already be positioning themselves around your life.

The perch also contains another layer of symbolism: surveillance. The bird of prey sitting high above the environment creates a psychological atmosphere. It communicates, "I see you." That is why predatory birds are associated with intimidation, dominance, and control. The presence alone alters behavior beneath it. Some blocker systems operate through this exact atmosphere. The goal is not immediate attack. The goal is constant pressure through awareness. A person feels watched, measured, tracked, psychologically managed, or continually forced into self-consciousness. In unhealthy systems, visibility itself becomes a tool of restraint.

On deliverance grounds people report feeling followed, by a *monitoring spirit* or what may be called, in some cultures, a *follow-follow spirit.*

This restraint can happen in individuals, in families, in churches, in workplaces, and in relationships. A person feels and may eventually learn they are being observed, evaluated, monitored emotionally, socially, financially, spiritually, or psychologically. The atmosphere itself becomes a perch system. The person modifies behavior because they know eyes are on them. Over time, they stop moving naturally. They stop flying instinctively. They stop exploring territory beyond the radius of approval, familiarity, or control.

There are people living far beneath the realm their gifts were designed to occupy because there is a predatory bird on the perch --, they may sense it even if they don't see it. Some people have become so accustomed to interruption, delay, smallness, emotional management, false systems, and controlled movement that true freedom now feels unfamiliar.

That is the tension many people feel when they begin awakening to misalignment. They cannot fully explain why certain environments suddenly feel too small, too controlled, too artificial, too psychologically managed, too spiritually restrictive. They become self-conscious. What once felt safe now feels limiting. What once felt structured now feels supervised. What once felt stabilizing now feels like managed containment.

The question becomes, even though you see the block, what is unseen about this block or on it? And if there is more than one thing, are those things working together? The visible block is often only the surface manifestation.

The real issue may be who positioned it, what feeds it? What agreement sustains it? What atmosphere empowers it? What fear protects it? What system benefits from it? What unseen attachment is connected to it? What is empowering whatever is perched on the perch?

The block itself may not be the only problem.

GOD'S GOT BLOCKS

In His own way, God may have said something like this to Jonah, "Jonah-- you will go no further in this wrong direction." Jonah is a profound example because the storm was not merely destruction. It was interruption, a forced interruption of wrongful movement.

God did not merely speak once and then shrug at Jonah's rebellion. The entire environment began resisting the direction Jonah had chosen. The sea itself became hostile to the journey. Movement was blocked. Progress became dangerous. The route destabilized.

The storm was not random chaos. It was directional opposition. Almost like Heaven saying, "You are not sailing peacefully into disobedience." Some Divine blocks are not there because God hates the person; they exist because the direction itself is destructive, misaligned, premature, rebellious, or outside assignment.

Jonah wanted to escape. God imposed interruption. Remember blocks are living, moving, active, strategizing. This block against Jonah escalated. First the storm. Then exposure. Then the casting of lots. Then confrontation. Then the sea. Then the fish (whale). Every stage progressively restricted the continuation of the wrong path. People often interpret escalating resistance only as enemy warfare when sometimes it can be Heaven refusing cooperation with a destructive direction.

The fish (whale) itself is fascinating symbolically because it was both judgment and preservation. Jonah was stopped, contained, hidden, restrained, carried, and preserved simultaneously. He was not allowed to continue the wrongful trajectory, but he was also not abandoned.

Look at God.

That is a completely different kind of "block" than pure destruction; that is corrective restraint.

"You will go no further in this wrong direction." Some blocks are not merely obstacles; they are verdicts against a trajectory. They are not necessarily rejection of the person, but rejection of the path.

In Balaam's case, we again see Divine obstruction. The block was present before the man fully perceived the danger. The donkey saw what Balaam did not. This is one of the most humbling realities in Scripture. It shows a person can be spiritually gifted, experienced, convinced they are proceeding correctly, and still be blind to what is standing in the path ahead.

Meanwhile the donkey keeps stopping, keeps turning aside. Keeps crushing against the wall. Keeps refusing forward movement. Balaam interprets resistance as irritation instead of protection.

In God's Mercy, sometimes the thing frustrating you is the very thing preventing destruction.

The narrow place between the walls is especially symbolic. The pathway becomes increasingly constrained until movement itself becomes impossible. The donkey literally presses Balaam's foot against the wall. The environment closes in.

Why?

Because the Angel with the drawn sword was ahead. Meaning, the narrowing was Mercy. The resistance was Mercy. The refusal was Mercy. The delay was Mercy. Balaam initially responded the way many people do when blocked, with anger, frustration, impatience, and accusation against the restraining thing. He struck the donkey because he believed the obstruction was the problem.

Blocks and barriers are present and that sometimes feels humiliating, inconvenient, slow, or frustrating. Sometimes it is the only thing standing between a person and catastrophe. Again, the block was directional. The Angel did not appear randomly in Balaam's kitchen; the obstruction appeared on the path.

It was about movement, trajectory, course, and direction. Balaam was between a rock and a hard place because Divine restraint can feel intensely uncomfortable when a person is determined to proceed.

The donkey had nowhere comfortable to go, not left, not right, and definitely not forward. The path itself became impossible. Yet impossibility was protection. The Balaam story is a very clear Biblical example that not every blockage is enemy opposition.

Some blocks are Mercy wearing the face of frustration. God's got blocks, but we don't kick against the goads.

One of the greatest mistakes people make when discussing blockers is assuming that every obstruction is demonic, malicious, unjust, or meant to be destroyed immediately. The Bible reveals something uncomfortable and deeply important: sometimes God Himself blocks movement.

Not every closed door is an attack. Not every delay is sabotage. Not every frustration is the enemy. Some blocks are protective. Some are corrective. Some are instructional. Some are merciful. Some exist because God sees what the person does not yet see. Human beings often pray for unrestricted movement without realizing unrestricted movement can become self-destruction in the wrong season, the wrong environment, direction, relationship, or condition of heart.

This is why discernment matters more than impulsive reaction.

The phrase "kick against the goads" is deeply revealing because a goad was not primarily meant to destroy the ox. It was meant to direct it, correct it, guide it, and to prevent harmful wandering. The resistance felt painful, but the purpose was guidance rather than annihilation.

Sometimes people spend enormous emotional energy fighting Divine restraint.

They push against Wisdom. They push against timing, conviction, boundaries and even closed doors. They push against correction from God. They may push against redirection, and waiting seasons. Some push against Truth, when it is uncomfortable. In their frustration they assume every form of resistance must automatically be removed. Remember life is not about you having your way all the time; it is the Lord's way that we are after.

Mature discernment asks a different question: Who placed the block there? What is the purpose of it?

If God is blocking something, fighting it may increase pain instead of producing freedom. Many people have exhausted themselves trying to force movement through doors God intentionally closed. Others have interpreted Mercy as punishment because restraint interrupted their desires. Human beings often desire movement without fully understanding destination.

Balaam is a profound example of this principle. He believed he was moving forward while an Angel of the Lord blocked the path ahead. The animal saw what the man did not see. Balaam became angry at the interruption because he misunderstood the purpose of the obstruction. He interpreted the block as frustration instead of protection. Had the obstruction not appeared, destruction would have followed.

This is why humility matters so deeply in seasons of resistance. Not every obstruction should be rebuked immediately. Some people rebuke what was sent to preserve them. Others call Wisdom warfare. Some call warfare Wisdom. Others call correction oppression. Others call restraint attack. Others call delay abandonment.

We must seek the plan of God in these moments, so we don't become so foolish as to oppose the Lord.

Scripture repeatedly shows God blocking movement for the purpose of protection, refinement, timing, redirection, or alignment. Paul was prevented from entering certain regions at certain times. Israel was delayed in wilderness seasons because internal conditions mattered as much as destination. Jonah encountered storms because movement itself was misaligned. Sometimes God blocks movement not because He hates the person, but because He loves them enough not to permit destruction unchecked.

This does not mean passively accepting every limitation forever. It does not mean abandoning discernment. Some blockers truly are destructive and must be confronted, removed, resisted, or navigated around. But spiritual maturity learns the difference between demonic obstruction and Divine restraint.

That difference often reveals itself through fruit.

Does the block eventually produce Wisdom, clarity, humility, Peace, alignment, maturity, repentance, preparation, or preservation? Or does it produce bondage, confusion, destruction, oppression, chaos, fragmentation, and death? One may be correction. The other may be attack.

The difficulty is that Divine blocks are often uncomfortable because they interfere with immediate desire. Human beings naturally want open movement, visible progress, quick answers, immediate fulfillment, and unrestricted access. But unrestricted access is not always love.

A parent who never restrains a child eventually destroys the child. A shepherd who never redirects sheep eventually loses them. A God who never blocks harmful movement would not be merciful. Sometimes the goad hurts because direction is changing.

Some people suffer unnecessarily because they continue kicking against what was meant to guide them. Pride fights restraint. Impulsiveness fights restraint. Ego fights restraint. Desire fights restraint. But Wisdom pauses long enough to ask whether the obstruction itself may contain instruction.

Mature people eventually learn that discernment is not merely knowing when to push forward. It is also knowing when to stop fighting the block and begin listening to why it exists.

Not every blockage is rejection. Sometimes it is redirection. Sometimes it is protection. Sometimes it is Mercy standing in the road before destruction arrives.

God's got blocks, but we don't kick against the goads.

HOW TO RECOGNIZE BLOCKERS

Without Losing Your Mind

Not every inconvenience is a blocker. Not every closed door is sabotage. Not every difficult person was assigned to destroy you. But some interruptions in life are more than random, and Wisdom requires us to notice patterns without surrendering our Peace.

Blockers, or evidence of blockers in a life can show up as repeated disruption at critical moments. Chronic diversion from purpose. Exhaustion without progress. Emotionally expensive relationships. Environments that consistently diminish clarity. Opportunities that repeatedly collapse the same way. Cycles of *almost*. Distraction before breakthrough. People who consume your momentum, and confusion attached to certain connections.

Healthy discernment notices patterns. Unhealthy paranoia assigns meaning to everything.

When you see patterns of repeated interruption and momentum disruption suspect Blockers. If you see motional drain, timing sabotage, cycles of *almost,* confusion attached to specific people/places/situations suspect blockers. Pray and ask God, Is it You, Lord? If it is, then proceed accordingly. If it is not God, then proceed accordingly.

Some blockers enter through flattery, attention, attraction, "help," urgency, fast opportunity and emotional dependency and they look like blessings.

But, are they?

Emotionally expensive people consume focus, drain clarity, create recovery cycles, bring confusion, interrupt momentum, and require constant emotional management.

Recognizing Blockers:

- repeated delays
- strange interruptions
- emotional exhaustion
- chronic detours
- false opportunities
- draining people
- confusion before progress
- timing sabotage

- “every time I get close…”

Many people miss blockers because they only evaluate isolated events instead of recurring patterns. A single interruption may mean nothing. A single delay may mean nothing. A single misunderstanding may mean nothing, so don’t lose your cool over any of that. But when the same types of disruption repeatedly appear around certain people, environments, situations, opportunities, or seasons, wisdom pays attention. Patterns matter. Repeated interruption matters. Momentum disruption matters. Cycles of *almost* matter.

Some people spend years standing at the edge of breakthrough while repeatedly getting pulled backward into the same emotional chaos, same distractions, same confusion, same instability, same entanglements, same delays, or same draining relationships. The issue is often not one isolated event. The issue is recurring interference around movement itself.

This is why blockers are often recognized through their effect on momentum.

A healthy relationship may require work, communication, compromise, maturity, patience, and growth, but it should not consistently destroy clarity, Peace, focus, purpose, discipline, or emotional stability. A healthy environment should not repeatedly produce confusion, exhaustion, emotional recovery cycles, or mental fragmentation. Some people normalize constant emotional turbulence because they have lived inside it so long, they no longer recognize it as obstruction.

One of the clearest signs of a blocker is repeated emotional drain attached to specific people, places, or situations.

There are environments where people consistently lose focus. There are conversations after which clarity disappears. There are relationships that consume enormous emotional energy while producing very little Peace, growth, stability, or healthy movement in return. Some people leave interactions feeling exhausted, inflamed, guilty, distracted, emotionally dysregulated, or mentally scattered every single time.

Emotionally expensive people are among the most difficult blockers to recognize because they often do not appear openly destructive. Many are intelligent, charming, wounded, attractive, charismatic, spiritual, helpful, funny, emotionally expressive, persuasive, or deeply compelling. Yet interacting with them consistently costs more than it produces.

They consume focus. They drain clarity. They create recovery cycles. They bring confusion. They interrupt momentum. They require constant emotional management.

Everything becomes about stabilizing their chaos, processing their emotions, rescuing their instability, responding to their emergencies, navigating their reactions, or recovering from their impact. Eventually entire portions of life become organized around managing their presence. I can recall too many conversations, some that went on from time to time for years as we tried to solve one person's 'problems.' As soon as one problem was solved, another cropped up. Every get together was to problem solving session for this person. I don't think she's ever got her life sorted out. Why should she, this is working, she's getting all the attention when the group gets together. That may be all she wants. Whether she realizes she is blocking others or not and wasting their time, I don't know. But she is being used as a blocker, even if she, herself doesn't orchestrate these problem-solving sessions.

This is why some people remain blocked for years without recognizing the source. They mistake emotional intensity for importance. They mistake emotional dependency for love. They mistake chaos for passion. They mistake exhaustion for loyalty. They mistake constant management for compassion.

Not every emotionally intense connection is healthy. Some people consume movement simply by consuming attention. This becomes even more dangerous when blockers arrive disguised as blessings. Some blockers enter through flattery. Others through attention. Some through attraction. Others through "help." Some through urgency. Others through fast opportunity. Others through emotional dependency.

Some don't enter at all, they just stand off and glare at you. You can almost see them silently vowing to stop you from your goals or assignments.

This is what makes discernment so important. Human beings naturally lower their guard around things that feel affirming, exciting, validating, comforting, attractive, useful, emotionally rewarding, or familiar. Many blockers do not arrive looking dangerous. They arrive looking beneficial.

Some opportunities are not opportunities at all. They are distractions wearing opportunity clothing.

A person may suddenly receive attention they have secretly longed for. They may feel chosen, admired, pursued, desired, emotionally seen, or validated. But over time, the "blessing" quietly begins consuming Peace, clarity, discipline, focus, stability, finances, purpose, time, emotional energy, or momentum. What initially felt exciting eventually becomes expensive.

Some blockers survive because people do not want to lose what is feeding their emotions. This is especially true in relationships. A person may recognize confusion, instability, manipulation, inconsistency, emotional exhaustion, or unhealthy attachment, but remain emotionally entangled because the connection still provides moments of affirmation, comfort, chemistry, attention, validation, fantasy, or emotional escape.

The blocker becomes emotionally rewarding enough to justify its damage. This is one reason discernment requires honesty.

Many people already recognize patterns long before they consciously admit them. They know which environments destabilize them. They know which people repeatedly consume Peace. They know which situations produce confusion. They know which patterns interrupt momentum. But honesty is uncomfortable because recognizing blockers often requires difficult decisions afterward.

Recognition creates responsibility. Clarity demands movement; so many people avoid clarity.

Timing sabotage is another important pattern to recognize. Some blockers consistently emerge near moments of transition, opportunity, clarity, rebuilding, healing, or advancement. Every time movement begins, disruption suddenly intensifies. Emergencies appear. Draining people reappear. Chaos increases. Confusion expands. Distraction multiplies. Emotional instability suddenly becomes urgent.

Again, this does not mean every inconvenience is spiritual warfare. Life itself contains unpredictability, difficulty, interruptions, and imperfect timing. Human beings must resist the temptation to become mystical about ordinary problems.

Healthy discernment notices patterns.

Unhealthy paranoia assigns meaning to everything.

Don't become so consumed with blockers that you stop functioning wisely altogether. Don't become suspicious of everyone. Don't interpret every disagreement as sabotage. Don't become emotionally reactive and spiritually exhausted. Ironically, paranoia itself eventually becomes another blocker; don't lose your cool.

Discernment should increase clarity, not destroy it. Discernment should produce Wisdom, not obsession. Discernment should produce Peace, not chronic suspicion. A mature person learns to observe fruit over time rather than reacting emotionally to isolated incidents. What consistently happens around certain people? What consistently happens in certain environments? What repeatedly interrupts movement? What repeatedly drains life, clarity, discipline, Peace, confidence, or momentum?

Patterns reveal what emotions often hide.

You can become aware of repeated obstruction without surrendering or becoming fearful of other people. Without losing your sanity, Peace, balance, or emotional stability in the process. Wisdom is calm enough to observe honestly. Wisdom is mature enough to acknowledge patterns. Wisdom is courageous enough to confront reality. Wisdom does not require hysteria in order to function.

Some blockers are real. Some patterns are real. Some disruptions are not random. But healthy discernment remains grounded enough to recognize blockers without allowing fear, suspicion, or obsession to become blockers themselves.

WHAT IS BLOCKING THIS?

Hidden Blockers

People can be working secretly against you. Sanballat and Tobias were working together against those who were trying to build, for example.

Haman was a blocker in plain sight, but you don't know blockers' agendas or their game plan. Often, they present as the opposite of what they really are.

When a blocker is a relative it is especially difficult to see. How could your little sister or younger brother? How could your own mother or other relation be praying diabolical prayers against you? How can people who you love and support and on whose side you are, also not be on your side and want the best for you?

One of the most unsettling realizations a person can have in life is discovering that not every smile is support, not every compliment is agreement, and not every person standing near you is standing with you. Some blockers are visible enemies. Others are hidden behind familiarity, affection, politeness, shared history, family bonds, or public cooperation. Some people work against movement quietly. They oppose subtly. They interfere indirectly. They delay strategically. They smile publicly while resisting privately.

This is why blockers are often difficult to identify. They rarely introduce themselves honestly.

Sanballat and Tobias did not initially arrive announcing themselves as enemies of restoration. They appeared around the rebuilding effort while carrying hidden agendas. The rebuilding of Jerusalem threatened something in them. The restoration of walls threatened their comfort, influence, and positioning. Not everyone celebrates rebuilding. Not everyone celebrates movement. Not everyone celebrates recovery. Some people benefit from your weakness, confusion, dependency, delay, or instability. The moment movement begins, opposition appears.

What makes blockers dangerous is not just their presence, but their concealment. Many blockers present as the opposite of what they truly are. They present as concern while spreading discouragement. They present as wisdom while producing fear. They present as friendship while sowing confusion. They present as helpers while draining momentum. They present as peacemakers while secretly inflaming division. They present as supporters while quietly resisting advancement behind the scenes.

Haman is a powerful example. His hatred did not begin openly; it developed internally long before it manifested publicly. One wounded ego became a strategic campaign against an entire people. That is how some blockers operate. What begins as jealousy, insecurity, pride, resentment, comparison, rejection, or offense quietly matures into resistance. Sometimes the person themselves may not even fully understand the depth of what is operating inside them. They simply become increasingly unable to celebrate your movement, your Peace, your growth, your healing, your favor, your opportunities, or your rebuilding.

This becomes even more painful when blockers exist inside circles where love is expected.

When it is strangers, the mind can process opposition more easily. People expect competition in business. People expect resistance from enemies. People expect jealousy from outsiders. But family creates emotional complications because family carries assumptions of loyalty, safety, shared identity, and protection. It is psychologically difficult to imagine that people you love deeply may not fully desire your advancement, especially if your advancement exposes their stagnation, insecurity, disappointment, bitterness, or unresolved wounds.

How could your little sister resent you? How could your younger brother compete with you? How could your own mother speak against you in prayer, in conversation, in spirit, or in attitude? How could people you help, support, defend, encourage, and protect quietly hope that you never move too far ahead of them? These questions are painful because they violate our emotional expectations about love and loyalty.

Many people spend years refusing to see what is directly in front of them because the truth feels emotionally unacceptable. Love can blind discernment. Familiarity can blind discernment. History can blind discernment. Shared blood can blind discernment. Sometimes people continue trusting harmful patterns simply because they cannot emotionally reconcile the possibility that someone close to them may be functioning as a blocker.

This does not mean Believers should become paranoid or suspicious of everyone around them. The goal is not emotional isolation. The goal is not fear. The goal is Wisdom. Not every difficult relative is an enemy. I'd be less likely to distrust the difficult ones rather than the quiet ones. Not every disagreement is sabotage. Families are complicated. Human beings are imperfect. People carry wounds, fears, insecurities, trauma, pride, and emotional immaturity. Sometimes people obstruct others without fully realizing the extent of what they are doing.

But to attain to Wisdom, one must eventually become honest.

There are people who become deeply uncomfortable when someone near them begins to grow, heal, mature, prosper, gain confidence, gain clarity, gain Peace, or gain momentum. Your movement confronts their lack of movement. Your rebuilding exposes their neglect. Your discipline exposes their excuses. Your healing exposes their refusal to heal. Your courage exposes their fear. Your obedience exposes their compromise.

Some blockers operate through direct attack. Others operate through subtle emotional manipulation. They drain focus. They create confusion. They manufacture guilt. They introduce discouragement. They monopolize emotional energy. They create unnecessary crises. They interrupt concentration. They compete, many times secretly. They resist indirectly. They withhold support while pretending neutrality. Sometimes they become strangely agitated whenever your real progress begins and your momentum increases.

One of the most painful realities in life is understanding that love is not always mutual in depth, purity, or intention. People may love you and still compete with you. People may care about you and still resent you. People may support you publicly and still hope privately that you do not surpass them. Human emotions are often conflicted and layered.

This is why discernment matters so deeply.

A wise person learns to observe fruit instead of merely listening to words. What consistently happens around certain people? What happens to your Peace, your focus, your clarity, your confidence, your opportunities, your discipline, your momentum, your emotional stability? Do confusion and discouragement always seem to increase? Does progress repeatedly stall? Do distractions multiply? Do you leave interactions drained, guilty, inflamed, fearful, exhausted, or uncertain? Patterns matter.

Jesus Himself understood hidden agendas. Judas walked closely among the Disciples while carrying betrayal internally, long before that betrayal manifested openly. Proximity is not proof of loyalty. Familiarity is not proof of agreement. Access is not proof of purity of heart.

Sometimes the most dangerous blockers are not the loudest enemies. Sometimes they are the people standing closest to the gate.

WHY WON'T THIS MOVE?

Environmental Blockers

Jericho wall, Red Sea, Jordan River and mountains that won't fall into the sea appear to be barriers to movement and progress.

Not all blockers are people. Some blockers are environmental. Some blockers are systems, structures, locations, conditions, atmospheres, or realities surrounding a person that make movement difficult, delayed, exhausting, or seemingly impossible. Environmental blockers do not always hate you personally. Some simply exist as massive realities standing between where you are and where you are trying to go.

One of the most frustrating experiences in life is standing in front of something that will not move.

You pray. You prepare. You try again. You push. You wait. You strategize. You obey. You hope. And still, the thing remains standing there. Unmoved. Unshaken. Unaffected by your effort. Some people know this feeling intimately. It is the feeling of staring at a wall, a system, a condition, a limitation, or a reality that appears larger than your present strength.

Scripture is filled with environmental blockers.

The children of Israel escaped Egypt only to find themselves trapped between Pharaoh's army and the Red Sea. This was not merely a personal problem; it was an environmental obstruction. The sea itself stood between bondage and movement. Water blocked freedom. Geography blocked progress. The people could see possibility ahead of them, but the environment itself prevented passage.

Environmental blockers often create emotional panic because they make people feel trapped. There appears to be no clear pathway forward and no safe pathway backward. Many people experience seasons exactly like this. Financially trapped. Emotionally trapped. Professionally trapped. Relationally trapped. Geographically trapped. Systemically trapped. The environment itself seems to oppose movement.

The Jericho wall represented another kind of environmental blocker. Massive. Fortified. Established. Intimidating. The wall did not just stand physically. It communicated psychological resistance. It told people, “You are not getting through here.” Some blockers speak without words. Institutions speak. Systems speak. Closed doors speak. Repeated rejection speaks. Delay speaks. A hostile environment can slowly train people to stop expecting movement altogether.

This is one of the greatest dangers of environmental blockers: over time they can reshape expectation. People begin adapting emotionally to obstruction. They stop imagining breakthrough. They stop preparing for movement. They stop believing the wall can fall. They stop believing the sea can part. They stop believing anything can change.

The Jordan River represented yet another type of blocker. Unlike the Red Sea, the Jordan stood between wilderness and inheritance. The people had already survived years of difficulty, but there was still another crossing before possession could occur. This is important because some people mistakenly believe that surviving hardship automatically means every barrier has already been removed. Sometimes major transitions still require crossing after years of preparation.

FYI: Sometimes the way you negotiate or navigate the barriers and blockers is telling about how you will maintain the new ground that you take. It is training.

Environmental blockers often intensify near transition points. The closer people come to movement, inheritance, rebuilding, healing, or purpose, the more obvious the obstruction may appear. The river looks impossible. The wall looks permanent. The mountain looks immovable. The system looks too established. The problem looks too large. The opposition looks too old.

This is where many people emotionally collapse.

Some become angry. Some become discouraged. Some retreat. Some become bitter. Some turn against God. Some attack themselves. Some begin fighting the wrong people. Others simply stop moving internally long before they stop moving physically.

Scripture repeatedly reveals a profound truth: not every environmental blocker is permanent. The Red Sea opened. The Jordan parted. The wall collapsed, and according to the Word of God, the mountain will be moved and fall into the sea if you command it in absolute faith. These are miracles and not because human strength was sufficient, but because God specializes in movement where movement appears impossible.

This does not mean every problem disappears instantly. It does not mean every mountain evaporates immediately. Sometimes God removes blockers miraculously. Sometimes He dismantles them gradually. Sometimes He leads people around them. Sometimes He strengthens people within them. Sometimes the environment changes. Sometimes the person changes. Sometimes both happen simultaneously.

What matters is refusing to surrender mentally before movement has even been attempted.

Many people are defeated long before the blocker itself defeats them. Fear magnifies the environment. Delay magnifies the environment. Repeated frustration magnifies the environment. Eventually people stop asking, "How do I move forward?" and begin asking, "Why even try?" That is the emotional goal of many blockers--, not to delay movement, but to destroy expectation.

Jesus addressed this mentality directly when He spoke about speaking to mountains. "Say to this mountain…" This statement is powerful because mountains represent environmental impossibilities. Large. Ancient. Established. Immovable. Mountains do not respond to ordinary human effort. They dominate landscapes. They shape environments. They alter movement itself.

Yet Jesus introduced the possibility that even environmental blockers are not beyond divine authority.

This was not permission for theatrical spirituality or denial of reality. Jesus was not teaching people to pretend mountains do not exist. He acknowledged their existence fully. The mountain was real. The obstruction was real. The difficulty was real. But He challenged the assumption that massive things are automatically permanent things.

Some people have spent so much time staring at blockers that they have unconsciously crowned them permanent.

The environment becomes godlike in the mind. The wall becomes absolute. The system becomes untouchable. The mountain becomes final. But Scripture repeatedly interrupts this mindset. Seas move. Walls fall. Rivers part. Mountains respond. Gates open. Prison doors release. Paths appear where none existed before.

Environmental blockers are real, but they are not always final.

Sometimes the greatest breakthrough in a person's life begins the moment they stop worshipping the size of the obstruction and start believing movement is still possible.

THE INVISIBLE BLOCKER

Agreement-Based Blockers

Soul ties. Emotional blockers.

Some blockers cannot be seen externally because they do not exist primarily in environments, systems, buildings, walls, or visible opposition. Some blockers exist through agreement. These blockers operate through connection, attachment, emotional alignment, loyalty, consent, access, desire, fear, dependence, or soul-level entanglement. They are often invisible to outside observers because nothing physical appears to be standing in the way. Yet movement remains blocked all the same.

Agreement-based blockers are among the most powerful blockers in human life because they operate internally while influencing external movement. A person may appear free while remaining emotionally tethered, mentally bound, spiritually conflicted, or psychologically attached to something that continues obstructing progress long after the visible relationship, situation, or environment has changed.

This is why some people cannot move forward even after physically leaving what harmed them.

The environment changed, but the agreement remained.

Soul ties are one of the clearest examples of agreement-based blockers. A soul tie is not merely emotional memory or ordinary affection. Human beings naturally remember people they loved, trusted, desired, admired, or shared life with. That alone is not bondage. But some connections penetrate deeper. They begin influencing thought patterns, emotional stability, decision-making, identity, desire, Peace, timing, self-worth, discernment, or movement itself. The relationship may be over physically while continuing psychologically, emotionally, spiritually, or internally.

This is why some people continue reacting to people who are no longer even present in their lives.

The invisible agreement remains active.

Agreement-based blockers often begin subtly. Few people consciously decide to become blocked. Instead, attachment forms gradually through repeated emotional investment, repeated exposure, repeated compromise, repeated desire, repeated dependence, repeated intimacy, repeated validation, or repeated surrender of discernment. Over time, what began as attraction becomes influence. What began as influence becomes attachment. What began as attachment becomes internal agreement.

This is why emotional blockers are often more difficult to recognize than visible opposition. A wall is easy to identify. A river is easy to identify. A hostile person is easy to identify. But emotional agreements frequently disguise themselves as love, loyalty, compassion, chemistry, understanding, destiny, connection, protection, or emotional safety.

Some people remain blocked because they are emotionally loyal to things that are destroying their movement.

An unhealthy relationship can become an invisible blocker. A toxic friendship, emotional dependency can become invisible blockers. Fear of abandonment can become an invisible blocker. Guilt can become an invisible blocker. Desire and fantasy can become invisible blockers. The need to feel chosen, wanted, admired, or emotionally secure can become an invisible blocker.

The difficulty with agreement-based blockers is that the person experiencing them often feels emotionally justified. The attachment feels real because the emotions are real. The longing is real. The pain is real. The chemistry is real. The history is real. The memories are real. But real emotions do not automatically produce healthy movement.

Some agreements block Peace. Others block clarity. Others block discipline. Some block purpose, while others block healing. Some block obedience. Others block discernment itself. A person can become so emotionally entangled that they begin protecting the very thing obstructing their future.

This is why some people repeatedly return to relationships, environments, or cycles that consistently damage them. The issue is no longer logic alone. Agreement has formed beneath the surface.

Agreement-based blockers also operate through identity. Some people internally agree with failure. Others agree with rejection. Others agree with limitation. Others agree with fear. Others agree with instability because instability has become familiar. A person can unconsciously align with narratives that obstruct movement for years. Don't say or internalize thoughts such as: "Nothing ever works out for me." "People always leave." "I will never succeed." "I always lose what I build." "I am not enough." Agreement with hopelessness can become a blocker all by itself.

This is why Scripture repeatedly emphasizes guarding the heart, renewing the mind, testing *spirits*, and discerning connections. Human beings are deeply shaped by what they continually agree with internally.

The danger of invisible blockers is that they often feel normal to the person carrying them. Emotional chaos can become normalized. Dysfunction, delay, and even pain can become normalized. Emotional obsession can become normalized. People adapt to blockage until they stop imagining freedom altogether.

Agreement-based blockers also explain why some people experience unusual confusion around certain individuals. Their judgment changes. Their discernment weakens. Their priorities shift. Their Peace disappears. Their clarity becomes unstable. They become emotionally reactive, impulsive, defensive, anxious, dependent, or consumed. Something deeper than ordinary interaction is occurring.

This does not mean every emotional connection is unhealthy. Human beings were created for relationship, intimacy, loyalty, friendship, love, covenant, and emotional connection. The goal is not emotional isolation or fear of attachment. The goal is discernment concerning what agreements are producing in your life.

Healthy agreement produces movement, Peace, clarity, maturity, stability, healing, Wisdom, Truth, and growth. Unhealthy agreement produces confusion, stagnation, emotional dependency, instability, exhaustion, obsession, compromise, or repeated cycles of pain.

Many invisible blockers remain active simply because the agreement itself has never been confronted honestly.

A person cannot break free from what they refuse to acknowledge. They cannot heal what they romanticize. They cannot move beyond what they continue protecting emotionally. Sometimes the invisible blocker is not the other person alone. Sometimes it is the internal agreement that still grants them access long after Wisdom should have closed the door.

This is why discernment matters so much; it is because not every strong feeling is guidance. Not every emotional pull is destiny. Not every attachment is healthy simply because it *feels* intense. Some things pull because they are aligned with purpose. Other things pull because they are entanglements.

Invisible blockers are dangerous precisely because they cannot always be seen externally. Yet some of the greatest delays in human life are not caused by visible walls, but by invisible agreements quietly operating beneath the surface of the heart.

SOMETHING IS IN THE WAY

Blockers Disguised as Protection

Hovering parents. False prophets and pastors can become blockers. There are people who never intended to can become blockers; and there are many who planned to. Either way, intentional or not, there are many who did.

Players who look like opportunities can end up being blockers. Shechem. David ruined Bathsheba's marriage. It's not like she had a choice; he was the king. The king calls, you show up or risk punishment or even death.

Amnon was a blocker. Judah blocked Tarmar, but later, Tamar outplayed Judah.

Some blockers are easy to identify because they arrive aggressively. They oppose openly. They attack visibly. Their resistance is direct and undeniable. But some of the most dangerous blockers in human life arrive disguised as protection, Wisdom, concern, love, spirituality, opportunity, or safety. These blockers are difficult to identify because they often appear beneficial on the surface while quietly obstructing growth, movement, maturity, healing, or destiny underneath.

Not everything that restricts movement is protecting you. Some things are simply controlling you.

This distinction matters deeply because human beings naturally lower their discernment around people and systems they believe are acting in their best interest. Protection creates trust. Guidance creates trust. Leadership and concern create trust. Spiritual authority creates trust. You can see from that list how false pastors or prophets are especially dangerous.

Family creates trust. Because trust lowers defenses, blockers disguised as protection often gain access more easily than obvious enemies ever could.

Hovering parents are one example. Protection, guidance and boundaries are all necessary in childhood. But some parents never emotionally release their children into adulthood because control has become intertwined with identity, fear, insecurity, loneliness, or emotional dependency. What begins as protection can insidiously transform into obstruction. The child cannot develop confidence because every decision is monitored. They cannot mature because risk is never permitted. They cannot build because independence is treated as betrayal. They cannot move because someone is constantly standing in front of the doorway and they think, for their own good.

Sometimes the parent sincerely believes they are protecting the child while unknowingly blocking development. Fear often disguises itself as wisdom. Anxiety often disguises itself as care. Emotional control often disguises itself as concern.

Spiritual environments can function similarly. False prophets and manipulative spiritual leaders often present themselves as protectors of God's people while quietly obstructing growth, freedom, discernment, and direct relationship with God. Some systems train people to fear independent thought, personal conviction, questioning, maturity, or spiritual confidence. Everything becomes filtered through the authority figure. Every decision requires approval. Every movement is monitored. Fear replaces discernment. Dependency replaces maturity.

Some spiritual blockers survive by convincing people that movement itself is dangerous.

This is one reason manipulation can thrive in religious settings. People naturally lower their defenses around individuals who appear spiritual, compassionate, anointed, wise, protective, or authoritative. Yet Scripture repeatedly warns that appearance alone is not proof of purity. Not every voice claiming to guide is actually leading toward freedom. Some voices lead toward dependence, fear, stagnation, confusion, exhaustion, or control.

People themselves can become blockers without fully realizing what they have become.

Some individuals begin as opportunities but gradually reveal themselves as obstruction. Some arrive appearing charming, exciting, supportive, romantic, helpful, connected, influential, or emotionally safe. They look like advancement. They feel like progress. They seem like answers. But eventually movement slows instead of increasing. Peace diminishes instead of growing. Clarity weakens. Stability disappears. Emotional chaos increases. Confusion expands. Recovery cycles become constant.

Some opportunities are actually detours.

Players often present themselves as opportunity because presentation is part of the strategy. Not everyone offering access intends covenant. Not everyone expressing desire intends responsibility. Some people enjoy pursuit more than building. Many players are there simply to defile with or without ulterior motives to that defilement. Sometimes they don't even know what will happen to the person they defile. Also, they don't realize what will happen to them as they too will be defiled in the defiling. Some enjoy access more than accountability. Some enjoy attention more than commitment. They create pull without intention to sustain what they are pulling toward themselves.

Scripture gives painful examples of this dynamic.

Shechem desired Dinah intensely, but desire alone did not produce righteousness, honor, or safety. Intensity is not proof of purity. Attraction is not proof of wisdom. Emotional pull is not proof of destiny. Human beings often confuse strong desire with trustworthy intention. Yet many people who create emotional pull are not prepared to carry the weight of what they are drawing toward themselves.

David's interaction with Bathsheba reveals another painful truth: powerful people can become blockers in the lives of others. Bathsheba did not initiate the situation. David's desire disrupted her marriage, endangered her household, and altered multiple lives permanently. It is easy to read biblical stories superficially and overlook the human complexity inside them. Bathsheba was placed into a situation where the power imbalance itself complicated choice. Sometimes blockers are people whose influence, authority, status, charisma, or access overwhelms the normal freedom of others.

Amnon reveals an even darker reality. Lust disguised itself as love. Obsession disguised itself as emotional need. Manipulation disguised itself as vulnerability. And once access was obtained, what pretended to be affection transformed into hatred. Some blockers do not merely delay movement. They wound identity, trust, confidence, Peace, and emotional safety itself.

This is why discernment matters more than attraction alone. Not everything pursuing you values you. Not everything desiring access intends covenant. Sometimes the person who loves your innocence will hate you when you are defiled, even if they are the one who defiled you.

Judah and Tamar reveal another dimension of blockers disguised as protection. Tamar had already lost one husband. Then another. Judah promised Shelah, his remaining son, but withheld him. Whether motivated by fear, suspicion, grief, superstition, or avoidance, the result was the same: Tamar remained trapped in suspended vulnerability. She was blocked from restoration. Blocked from fruitfulness. Blocked from security. Blocked from movement forward as a barren widow waiting on promises that were ot being fulfilled.

This is one of the most frustrating forms of blockage: indefinite delay disguised as eventual provision.

"Later" becomes obstruction. "Wait" becomes obstruction. "Soon" becomes obstruction.

Some people never intend to fulfill what they continue promising. Delay itself becomes the mechanism of control.

Tamar eventually recognized that passive waiting would leave her permanently trapped. She understood something critical: some blockers are not removed through endless compliance. Some systems only continue functioning because everyone inside them agrees to remain passive. Tamar outmaneuvered the system blocking her future. The situation itself is morally complicated, but the principle remains powerful: there are moments in life when a person must recognize that what appears to be protection, process, leadership, or delay has actually become obstruction.

This chapter is not permission for rebellion, recklessness, paranoia, or rejection of all authority. Healthy protection exists. Wise counsel exists. Loving leadership exists. Responsible parenting, Godly spiritual guidance exists. Genuine care really does exist. Not every restriction is manipulation, and every delay is not obstruction. Sometimes protection really is protection.

Wisdom asks an important question: *what is the fruit?*

Does the relationship produce maturity or dependency? Does the guidance produce clarity or fear? Does the system produce growth or stagnation? Does the protection eventually release people into movement, or does it imprison them inside limitation? True protection prepares people for movement. False protection becomes the thing standing in the way.

NOTHING IS MOVING

The presence of blockers explains *why movement still isn't happening even after awareness arrives.* You should ask God, but you'd be surprised how many blockers have been sent into your life to present as obstacles to your progress in life. Blocking anything from relationships to careers to even investment of financial opportunities that present as blockers.

Not everything announces itself as an enemy. Some things arrive looking reasonable, necessary, romantic, urgent, helpful. They can be flattering and showing up as once in a lifetime opportunity. But really, their assignment is blockage.

Blockers that consume time, drain focus, redirect energy, create delay, distort judgment can keep a person emotionally occupied. They can exhaust finances, and derail momentum. They create recovery cycles. The scary part? Some blockers don't stop you by attacking you.

They stop you by engaging you.

Some blockers were never sent to destroy you. They were only sent to keep you occupied long enough to delay what was supposed to happen. Some people are not in your life to build with you. They are standing in the doorway of your next season. A blocker does not always appear as resistance. Sometimes it appears as distraction.

This is beyond "haters"; haters can hate you and never take action in the physical against you. This is different. There are draining relationships, fake emergencies, emotionally expensive people, love bombers, gaslighters, seductive detours. There are wrong environments and cycles of loss, destruction or stagnancy. There is addiction, confusion, performance, chronic instability. Endless unfinished projects can detour you too. When looking at opportunities that consume but never produce you will see blockers.

So structurally it looks like: Block → Block → Block → Block, Each one is linked to the previous one. The word "block" there does NOT mean obstruction. It means a unit/container of stored information. Systems form. Patterns connect. Obstruction compounds. cycles reinforce themselves. This is oddly similar to how linked systems operate in a blockchain: one connected structure affecting the next.

These blocks are chained together, they are dependent upon one another, like a network, although they may not be physically connected. A sophisticated connection of blockades like this can create siege-like conditions.

Isolated blockers connect to create interconnected blocking systems. Siege is not always one enemy standing in front of one door. A siege is sustained restriction, coordinated pressure, interrupted supply, blocked movement, exhausted resources, psychological wearing-down, and encirclement.

The "blocks" may not appear physically connected while still functioning cooperatively. That happens constantly in real life. Because of connected blockades a person could be suffering emotional exhaustion, financial instability, chronic distraction, toxic relationships, workplace stress, sleep deprivation, spiritual confusion, family pressure, performance culture, and fear.

These things may not seem directly connected, but together, they create systemic obstruction. A person under siege often experiences no room to recover, no clear movement, constant interruption, resource depletion, psychological fatigue, emotional erosion, reduced clarity, reduced hope, and reduced capacity.

In a siege, sometimes no single blocker appears catastrophic by itself. It is the cumulative pressure that is strategized to create collapse. Some people are not facing one blocker; they are experiencing coordinated obstruction.

Siege works by exhausting movement over time. A blockade does not always stop you instantly. Sometimes it slowly reduces your ability to move.

These linked systems reinforce one another. One blockage strengthens another, exhaustion weakens discernment. Weakened discernment invites bad decisions which increase instability. This increases fear which reduces movement. See the cascade here? Reduced movement creates stagnation. Now the person is inside a reinforcing obstruction cycle.

PRETTY BLOCKERS

That phrase is dangerous in the BEST way because it instantly communicates that not everything blocking you looks ugly. Some blockers arrive attractive, handsome, charming, polished, intelligent, luxurious, comforting, validating, exciting or emotionally intoxicating. Because they are beautiful, people do not recognize them as obstruction.

Of course, the devil would send in seductive distractions, especially those who know how to stroke a man's ego. Especially to those who are themselves vain. Blockers create emotionally addictive relationships and present flattering opportunities. This is all about image-driven living, status, and performance. They recognize aesthetics over purpose, creating stunning, beautiful relationship prisons. These are intoxicating, pleasant detours. The stagnation that results from it is real. It's glamorous, but it is still stagnation.

Spiritually? This is very deep because Scripture repeatedly shows attractive obstruction. Desirable but destructive things. Beauty disconnected from Wisdom (Solomon). Appearance masking danger, Absalom.

Delilah, a beautiful woman from the wrong 'tribe' that Samson's parents tried to discourage him from. Delilah wanted all the wrong things from Samson, and got it.

Absalom, by description maybe the most beautiful man in the Bible.

The fruit in Eden on the forbidden tree described by the devil as *good to look at.*

Vanity structures, beautiful people--, image worship. Some blockers are not ugly enough to reject immediately.

The danger of pretty blockers is that people protect them instead of removing them. Pretty privilege is a real thing.

Still in the background or the foreground depending on how you look at it, the defilement, which we have discussed in the last chapter. Defilement and the iniquity of it will block for a long time or forever if you never realize the connection and repent of it.

People cling harder to blockers that: comfort them, validate them, entertain them, beautify their image, reduce loneliness, feed ego, and create fantasy.

Witches aren't always wearing black, conical hats and have long noses with a wart at the tip. Some are very beautiful. Wouldn't a witch want to be pretty to be more attractive? How do we know that's not what led them into witchcraft—image? To get pretty privilege. To get favor or to be accepted into situations with few or no questions?

What do you think that person is sitting on the block for? To assess their handiwork? To see if their plan is working? To watch their victim struggle or suffer?

BLOCKERS AT THRESHOLDS

Why Certain Doors Never Open

Strongmen. Gatekeepers. Elders at the Gates.

Not every blocker appears in the middle of the road. Some stand at thresholds.

The closer a person comes to transition, movement, authority, elevation, healing, freedom, visibility, restoration, or purpose, the more resistance may appear concentrated around the doorway itself. Thresholds matter because thresholds represent change. Crossing them means leaving one realm and entering another. It means identity shifts. Access shifts. Authority shifts. Atmospheres shift. Some people are not resisted because they are moving; they are resisted because they are approaching something.

Throughout history, gates represented power. Cities were governed at gates. Elders sat at gates. Legal matters were decided at gates. Commerce moved through gates. Protection existed at gates. Access was controlled there. Gates were not decorative structures. They were systems of permission, authority, and transition. Whoever controlled the gate often controlled movement itself.

This is why threshold blockers feel so intense. A person may move relatively unhindered for a season and suddenly encounter confusion, exhaustion, fear, delay, sabotage, strange resistance, emotional upheaval, distraction, relational chaos, or psychological warfare right before breakthrough, right before clarity, right before healing, right before change. The pressure gathers near the entrance.

In spiritual language, people often describe these forces as strongmen or gatekeepers. Whether understood literally, symbolically, psychologically, structurally, or spiritually, the pattern itself is undeniable: certain transitions attract concentrated resistance. There are systems that benefit from keeping people in familiar territory. Some structures survive only if people never cross into greater freedom, maturity, clarity, authority, or alignment.

A stronghold does not merely imprison; it preserves an existing order. A gatekeeper does not necessarily destroy a person; the gatekeeper controls passage. The message becomes, "You may approach, but you will not enter." Many people live in cycles of almost because they continually arrive at thresholds but retreat under pressure. Fear rises. Fatigue rises. Old appetites return. Old relationships reappear. Distractions multiply. Internal instability intensifies. The closer they get to crossing over, the louder resistance becomes.

Threshold blockers are often deeply psychological as well. Some people have spent so long adapting to one realm that the doorway into another feels threatening. Freedom can feel unfamiliar. Peace can feel suspicious. Stability can feel unnatural. Visibility can feel dangerous. A person may unconsciously sabotage access to the very thing they prayed for because crossing the threshold requires becoming someone new.

This is why discernment matters at doors. Not every closed door should be forced open. Some gates protect. Some barriers preserve life. But there are also illegitimate blockages—systems of fear, manipulation, confusion, pride, control, trauma, intimidation, or spiritual oppression that attempt to keep people perpetually outside their rightful place. These systems often operate through weariness and discouragement rather than obvious destruction. If the person can be exhausted long enough, delayed long enough, entangled long enough, they may eventually stop approaching the gate altogether.

The tragedy is that many people turn back at the threshold without realizing how close they were to crossing over. Resistance intensified not because the path was wrong, but because the doorway mattered.

Every threshold asks a question, Who are you once you pass through this gate? Crossing thresholds changes more than location. It changes identity, access, expectation, responsibility, and range. Some blockers exist because something beyond the threshold threatens the existing order. Once a person crosses certain gates, they cannot fully return to who they were before.

That is why threshold warfare feels different. It is not merely about movement. It is about access.

THE COST OF LEAVING BLOCKERS UNMOVED

There is a cost to leaving blockers unmoved. What you don't remove today will come back to bite tomorrow.

Inherited blockers, for example: your kids will have to fight those giants that you don't remove today.

Not every blocker disappears simply because time passes. Some remain in place for generations because nobody confronts them directly. What is tolerated today often becomes inherited tomorrow.

One of the greatest mistakes people make is assuming that unresolved obstruction remains contained to their own life. It rarely does. Patterns spread. Atmospheres spread. Systems spread. Fear spreads. Dysfunction spreads. Unchallenged strongholds often become normalized structures passed from one generation to the next until descendants begin fighting battles they never created.

Scripture repeatedly shows this principle through nations, families, leadership systems, idols, enemies, and territories left unconfronted. Giants not removed in one generation reappeared in another. Enemies tolerated in one season became oppression later. What should have been dismantled became embedded. That is the danger of inherited blockers.

Some people think only in terms of personal comfort. They think, "Can I survive this?" "Can I manage this?" "Can I work around this?" "Can I adapt to this?" But the deeper question is, "What happens if this remains standing?"

Many blockers grow stronger through accommodation. The longer something remains unchallenged, the more normal it begins to feel. Entire families can organize themselves around dysfunction. Entire bloodlines can adapt to fear, chaos, addiction, secrecy, emotional instability, poverty thinking, manipulation, passivity, rage, performance systems, or cycles of brokenness until the abnormal becomes familiar.

Children raised around blockers often learn coping before freedom. They learn navigation instead of removal. They learn survival instead of authority. They inherit emotional maps built around avoidance, silence, fear, appeasement, or limitation. Then years later they find themselves exhausted by battles that existed long before they arrived. This is why unresolved giants matter.

A giant left standing does not usually remain passive. What intimidates one generation often pursues the next. The cost of delayed confrontation compounds over time. What begins as compromise can become bondage. What begins as avoidance can become inheritance.

Inherited blockers are not always dramatic. Sometimes they appear as recurring ceilings: the same financial collapse, the same relational dysfunction. We may see the same emotional instability, the same fear of visibility, the same cycles of self-sabotage, the same inability to sustain Peace, over and again. We may see the same attraction to chaos, the same tolerance for manipulation, the same resistance to growth in the child that was in the parents and the ancestors.

People often call these "family patterns" without realizing how deeply entrenched some systems become when not dealt with, but left unmoved.

This does not mean every struggle is demonic or generational in a sensationalized sense. Sometimes inherited blockers are psychological, relational, cultural, environmental, or learned behaviors reinforced over decades. Regardless of the source, the principle remains: what is not confronted often continues.

The tragedy is that many people spend their lives adjusting to things they were meant to dismantle. There comes a point where survival is no longer enough. Somebody must decide, “This stops here.”

The children should not have to spend their strength fighting giants that should have been removed long ago. However, that pattern appears repeatedly in Scripture. The issue was often not merely military failure; it was incomplete removal.

Where God said, "completely destroy the enemy" (but they did not). The people would win enough to survive, but not enough to eliminate the source of future oppression. That’s like stopping your antibiotics because you feel better, but not finishing the course, to get rid of ALL the bacteria.

Partial obedience often creates recurring warfare. God would warn them not to leave certain enemies, idols, altars, systems, or influences in place because what remains embedded eventually regains influence. But the people frequently chose compromise, forced labor instead of removal, coexistence instead of separation, management instead of dismantling. At first, it probably looked practical, merciful, economical, or harmless.

Later it became a snare. A snare is something left in place that eventually entangles movement, loyalty, worship, Peace, identity, or direction. There are too many long-term blockages that begin as tolerated remnants, or things not fully removed. They will be seen as things not fully confronted or not fully severed. People often want peaceful coexistence with things that eventually war against them.

That is one of the great themes running through the entire Book of Judges, cycles repeated because of previous corruption, compromise, or enemies remained in the land. The unfinished battle became inherited instability. Some things cannot simply be managed, visited occasionally, kept "under control," or left dormant in the corner. Dormant is not dead. Eventually the next generation encounters what the previous generation merely tolerated. Your kids will have to fight those giants that you don't remove today. Unresolved obstruction rarely stays isolated to one season. What remains will eventually speak again.

YOU KEEP HITTING SOMETHING

Self as a Blocker

Lord, protect me from self-sabotage.

One of the most frustrating experiences in life is repeatedly approaching movement only to encounter resistance at the exact moment breakthrough seems near. Some people live with the constant feeling that they keep hitting something they cannot fully see. Every time progress begins, something interrupts it. Every time Peace starts forming, confusion emerges. Every time stability appears possible, disruption arrives. Every time opportunity opens, something blocks access before movement fully materializes. Many people assume these patterns are random, but repeated obstruction at thresholds often reveals something deeper.

Thresholds are important places in Scripture. Gates matter. Doors matter. Crossings matter. Entry points matter. Transitions matter. Many blockers intensify near moments of movement because thresholds represent change. Thresholds represent movement from one state into another. From bondage into freedom. From wilderness into inheritance. From obscurity into visibility. From dependence into maturity. From instability into Peace. From limitation into expansion.

This is why resistance often intensifies at doors.

Many people are not attacked most heavily in the middle of stagnation. They encounter heightened resistance near movement. Near clarity. Near healing. Near obedience. Near rebuilding. Near breakthrough. Near transition. Near new environments. Near restoration. Near freedom.

You keep hitting something.

The frustration of threshold blockers is that the person often knows that movement is possible. They can see the door. They can see the opportunity. They can see the next level. They can feel change approaching. Yet something repeatedly interferes before crossing fully occurs.

Some people experience this relationally. Others financially. Others spiritually. Others emotionally. Others professionally. Others mentally. A person may repeatedly approach stability while remaining unable to fully enter it. They may repeatedly begin healing while continually returning to old wounds. They may repeatedly start building while constantly losing momentum. They may repeatedly approach opportunity while consistently becoming distracted, entangled, delayed, discouraged, emotionally inflamed, or destabilized before arrival.

At some point, Wisdom begins praying honestly. "Lord, protect me from self-sabotage, in the Name of Jesus, Amen."

That prayer matters because not all blockers are external. Sometimes the thing standing at the threshold is internalized fear, emotional immaturity, unresolved trauma, pride, addiction to chaos, fear of success, fear of responsibility, fear of visibility, or fear of change itself. Some people unconsciously destroy what they prayed for because movement requires becoming someone they are not yet emotionally prepared to be.

Self-sabotage is one of the most painful blockers because the person often does not fully recognize their own participation in the cycle. They repeatedly choose what damages them. They repeatedly reopen closed wounds. They repeatedly return to what drains them. They repeatedly destroy Peace through impulsive decisions, emotional reactions, poor discernment, unhealthy agreements, ungoverned appetite, or refusal to mature. Then they wonder why every door seems to close.

Sometimes the enemy outside is not the only enemy involved.

Scripture repeatedly shows the importance of gates and gatekeepers. Reiterating from earlier: Elders sat at gates. Authority operated at gates. Decisions, commerce, and protection happened at gates. Access was monitored at gates. Gates determined movement in and movement out. This is why gatekeeping is such a powerful Biblical image. Whoever controls gates often controls access.

Strongholds and strongmen operate similarly. A strongman does cannot attack randomly. A strongman occupies territory. It guards regions. It establishes dominance and resists removal. Some blockers become deeply entrenched systems in families, communities, cultures, institutions, or generations. Fear becomes entrenched. Poverty becomes entrenched. addiction becomes entrenched. Violence, chaos, secrecy, emotional instability, as well as dysfunction can all become normalized because the blocker has occupied the territory so long that people begin adapting to it instead of removing it. Inherited blockers are so serious.

Some individual and family struggles existed long before a person arrived. Families can pass down patterns, fears, wounds, addictions, dysfunctions, limitations, and destructive agreements for generations. Sometimes children inherit not only genetics and traditions, but unfinished battles. The giant someone refused to confront decades earlier still stands in the path years later.

What people tolerate repeatedly becomes established.

This is why the Bible emphasizes removing destructive influences fully instead of partially. What remains alive eventually regains strength. What is ignored often returns larger later. What is excused repeatedly becomes normalized. Many people delay confronting blockers because confrontation feels uncomfortable in the present, but unresolved obstruction rarely simply disappears.

What you do not remove today may become tomorrow's greater battle. A compromise ignored becomes a pattern. A pattern ignored becomes a stronghold. A stronghold ignored becomes inheritance. Then eventually children grow up fighting giants they never created.

This happens emotionally. Financially. Spiritually. Relationally. Psychologically. Entire generations can inherit fear, scarcity thinking, rage, addiction, silence, instability, distrust, emotional fragmentation, victimhood, or cycles of destruction simply because nobody removed the blocker when it first appeared.

The cost of leaving blockers unmoved is often delayed rather than immediate. That delay deceives people. Because the consequences are not instant, people assume the issue is harmless. Blockage, delay, and dysfunction compounds over time. Entanglement compounds over time. A person may tolerate a small obstruction for years only to discover later that the obstruction shaped the entire direction of their life.

This is why discernment requires courage. Some things must be confronted early before they mature into systems. Some doors never open because something unresolved is still occupying the gate. Some people repeatedly ask God for movement while protecting the very thing obstructing movement. Others demand new territory while refusing to remove old agreements. Some want inheritance without warfare. Others want Peace without confrontation. But many thresholds require honesty before crossing.

The goal is not paranoia or obsession with darkness. The goal is awareness. The goal is understanding that repeated impact against the same invisible wall may indicate that something deeper requires attention.

You keep hitting something for a reason.

Sometimes breakthrough begins not when the door changes, but when the blocker finally gets moved.

A LION IN THE PATH

Yes, sometimes there really is a lion in the road. Sometimes the lion is real, and sometimes it is perceived.. Sometimes the lion is the story we tell ourselves to avoid movement. Fear has blocked more people than failure ever will.

In the case of real peril, some blockers are dangerous. There are many predatory people. There are destructive systems. People endure spiritual attacks, exploitation and deception. Spiritual violence as well as violence in the natural are real hurdles. Then there is excuse & avoidance saying, "There is a lion in the streets." That's when fear becomes justification for paralysis. Here the blocker is fear, exaggeration, avoidance, procrastination, and imagined catastrophe.

There is a difference between legitimate caution and immobilizing fear. Sometimes there really is a lion in the road.

That distinction matters because Wisdom requires balance. Some people move through life recklessly, pretending danger does not exist. Others become so consumed by fear that they stop moving altogether. Both extremes create destruction. Mature discernment learns the difference.

Scripture presents one of the most revealing pictures of this tension in Proverbs: "There is a lion in the streets." The statement itself is fascinating because it may or may not be true. The danger could be real. The lion could actually be present. But the deeper issue in the proverb is paralysis. Fear becomes justification for remaining unmoving, inactive, stagnant, hidden, avoidant, or unwilling to engage life.

Many blockers in life are legitimate dangers. Predatory people exist. Manipulative systems exist. Exploitation exists. Spiritual attack exists. Violence and sabotage are real. Deception exists. Human beings are not called to blind naivety. Wisdom recognizes danger. Wisdom recognizes patterns. Wisdom recognizes unsafe environments, dishonest people, destructive relationships, corrupt systems, and situations that require caution, boundaries, or withdrawal.

Some lions are dangerous. Some are toothless.

There are environments where people are exploited emotionally, financially, spiritually, or physically. There are individuals who intentionally manipulate others for pleasure, profit, control, ego, power, or access. Some people prey on vulnerability itself. Others build systems that quietly consume the lives, Peace, labor, finances, confidence, or futures of those trapped inside them. Not every warning is paranoia. Not every fear is irrational. Some threats are genuine.

This is why discernment must never become simplistic positivity. Telling people to ignore danger is not Wisdom. Scripture itself repeatedly warns about wolves, serpents, deception, traps, snares, false prophets, corrupt rulers, thieves, and predatory behavior. Jesus told His followers to be wise as serpents and harmless as doves because Wisdom acknowledges that danger exists in the world.

Fear creates a different kind of blocker when caution transforms into paralysis.

This is where the lion in the street becomes symbolic. At some point, fear itself begins obstructing movement more than the actual danger. A person becomes so focused on what *could* happen that they stop living, building, risking, trusting, moving, speaking, growing, healing, trying, loving, or obeying. The possibility of failure becomes more powerful than the desire for movement.

Fear has blocked more people than failure ever will.

Many people never discover what could have been built because imagined catastrophe convinced them not to begin. Others remain trapped in cycles they hate because fear exaggerated the danger of change. Some stay emotionally attached to destructive relationships because the unknown feels more frightening than dysfunction. Others never pursue purpose because fear magnifies rejection, embarrassment, loss, criticism, or uncertainty until movement feels unbearable.

Fear is one of the most convincing storytellers in human life. It exaggerates. It predicts disaster. It magnifies consequences. It whispers worst-case scenarios repeatedly until imagination itself becomes a blocker. A person can become imprisoned by things that have not even happened. Sometimes the lion exists only in anticipation.

This is why procrastination is often deeper than laziness. Many people are not inactive because they lack desire. They are inactive because fear has attached itself to movement. If they start, they may fail. If they speak, they may be rejected. If they trust, they may be hurt. If they leave, they may regret it. If they build, they may lose it. If they succeed, they may become visible. If they move forward, life itself may change.

Eventually avoidance begins disguising itself as Wisdom.

Some people call fear discernment. Others call avoidance patience. Others call procrastination preparation. Others endlessly research, analyze, hesitate, discuss, postpone, and imagine until movement dies completely. The lion in the street becomes the permanent explanation for why nothing ever changes.

Legitimate caution protects movement. Immobilizing fear destroys movement. Legitimate caution says, "Be wise." Immobilizing fear says, "Do not move at all." Legitimate caution prepares. Fear paralyzes. Legitimate caution recognizes danger while still allowing life to continue. Fear turns danger into identity. A fearful person eventually sees lions everywhere.

This is one reason unresolved fear becomes spiritually dangerous. Over time, fear distorts perception.. Neutral situations begin feeling threatening. Opportunities begin feeling unsafe. Relationships begin feeling dangerous. Doors begin feeling suspicious. Change begins feeling catastrophic. The person no longer responds to reality accurately because fear has magnified the possibility of harm beyond proportion.

Some people become blocked not because every lion is imaginary, but because they no longer know the difference between real danger and perceived danger.

This is where courage becomes essential. Courage is not denial. Courage is not pretending fear does not exist. Courage is movement in the presence of uncertainty. Courage allows discernment without surrendering to paralysis. Courage asks wise questions while still remaining willing to move when movement is necessary.

David faced real lions. Daniel faced real lions. Samson faced real lions. Scripture never denies danger. But neither does it glorify fear.

Many people wait for the complete absence of risk before obeying God, moving forward, changing environments, building, loving, speaking, trusting, creating, healing, or beginning again. That day rarely comes. He who observes the wind will never sow. Life itself contains uncertainty. Movement contains vulnerability. Faith requires motion despite incomplete visibility. Sometimes the lion in the path must be avoided. Sometimes the lion must be confronted. Sometimes the lion is exaggerated by fear. Sometimes the lion is the excuse people repeat because remaining still feels emotionally safer than movement. Wisdom learns the difference.

Many people become free the moment they realize the thing stopping them is no longer the lion itself, but the fear of movement created by constantly staring at it.

Technology has become a modern gatekeeper for many people. Many jobs, and even basic daily tasks increasingly require some level of digital navigation. Yet many people freeze emotionally the moment a computer, software platform, online form, password reset, upload screen, or unfamiliar interface appears or is mentioned. The issue is not intelligence; it is fear. Technology becomes the lion. Some immediately look for someone else to take over rather than pushing through learning it. .

This avoidance becomes expensive. Some pay others to complete simple digital tasks they could learn themselves with patience and repetition, losing money, confidence, and opportunity. Some blockers are not removed; they are navigated. At some point a person must decide whether they will remain blocked by the interface or develop the capacity to move through it.

Some blockers are external, some are internal, inherited, spiritual, relational, psychological, imagined, exaggerated. When fear is internalized, it is very strong.

MONEY BLOCKERS

Money blockers can make you miss anything from a job opportunity to investment options. They can do this by evil entanglements. Unauthorized access, mismatch, deception and mask. Defilement is big in causing people to have cycles of having and then losing. Relatives? Sometimes. Co-workers. Co-eds. Some strangers are blockers and specifically money blockers.

The plan of money blockers can be to have its victim "lack money," but most of the time it is more selfish than that. They desire to have money and have not given a thought as to whether you will have any or not.

Money blockers can often be systems, beliefs, fear, shame, chaos. Error can lead you into poor timing. Emotional chaos can cause reckless spending and make you a candidate for both manipulation and dependency.

If you have been a victim of scarcity conditioning, financial confusion, sabotage, or endless emergencies (families are famous for this one) then you have been confronted by money blockers. A person could be blocked and have limited to no ability to retain resources.

Structural Money Blockers are the external conditions and built-in disadvantages that can keep a person struggling even when they are willing to work, pray, save, and be responsible. Debt systems, exploitative environments, ongoing instability, lack of access, broken infrastructure, and predatory relationships can all function like cages around financial progress. Some people are not careless with money; they are trapped inside systems that continuously drain it.

When transportation breaks down, opportunities are missed. When the environment is unstable, planning becomes difficult. When access to healthy work, fair wages, safe housing, sound financial tools, or trustworthy support is limited, progress slows before it even begins. Structural blockers matter because they remind us that financial struggle is not always the result of poor character. Sometimes the structure itself is arranged to consume momentum, making it harder to build, keep, and multiply resources.

Emotional Money Blockers operate beneath the surface, but they can be just as powerful as poverty, debt, or low wages. Guilt around prosperity can make a person feel wrong for having more, while fear of success can cause them to shrink back from opportunities that would require greater visibility, responsibility, or change. Self-sabotage may show up in poor timing, impulsive decisions, or walking away from what was beginning to work. Overspending for validation turns money into a tool for emotional approval rather than wise stewardship.

An inability to say no keeps resources leaking toward demands that should have been refused. Rescue addiction drains finances through the constant need to save others, fix other people's crises, or prove love through sacrifice. Emotional money blockers are dangerous because they disguise themselves as compassion, humility, generosity, or even loyalty while quietly weakening financial stability.

Relational Money Blockers show up through the people attached to your life and the patterns they help create around money. Draining people can absorb time, focus, Peace, and resources without ever helping build anything in return. Financial manipulation can appear through guilt, pressure, control, dishonesty, hidden motives, or emotional tactics meant to keep someone giving, spending, or covering what they should not have to cover. Constant dependency cycles create an atmosphere where one person is always rescuing and another is always in crisis.

Sometimes partners or family members repeatedly destroy progress through chaos, irresponsibility, resentment, sabotage, or bad decisions that undo what has just been built. There are even households where every time a person starts saving, some new emergency, demand, or manufactured obligation appears to consume it. Relational money blockers matter because not all financial warfare is about numbers on paper; sometimes it is about who has access to your life, your energy, your wallet, and your decisions.

Internal Money Blockers are the habits, thought patterns, and inner weaknesses that quietly interfere with financial stewardship. Lack of discipline can make good intentions collapse under pressure. Avoidance keeps people from opening bills, checking balances, making plans, or facing what must be dealt with. Disorganization creates unnecessary loss because money slips through gaps, deadlines are missed, and important details are neglected. Fear of responsibility can make a person resist the very growth they say they want because increase also requires management.

Confusion clouds judgment, weakens timing, and leaves a person vulnerable to bad choices or manipulation. Fantasy thinking replaces practical stewardship with wishful ideas, emotional optimism, or unrealistic expectations that never become structure. Internal money blockers are often the hardest to confront because they do not feel like enemies at first. Yet until they are recognized, they can stay hidden and undermine opportunity, retention, and long-term financial Peace.

Spiritual Money Blockers are such as greed, idolatry, performance, bondage to image, pride, disobedience, and chronic instability, on one side. On the other, spiritual money blockers are things sent in the unseen world to siphon, block, draw or compromise a person so siphoning can happen. Don't fall for these traps.

Some people do not have a money problem. They have a retention problem. Some people know how to receive money. They do not know how to keep momentum. (Read my books, ***When Not Having Money Is Not About Money***, or the book, **STRUCTURE**.) I contend that if you don't know which altars the people you are involved with are involved with, then you need to break all connections especially those that concern money.

Almost everyone has experienced some form of financial obstruction. These are household patterns, agreements, systems, and cultures that quietly sustain lack, instability, stagnation, or financial blockage. Four hidden poverty altars in the average home.

When the household altar of chaos rules you see that nothing is organized. Nothing is maintained. Bills are ignored. There are constant emergencies. There is impulsivity. Ther is no structure. There is no stewardship, and no Peace. This altar consumes momentum because disorder constantly leaks energy and money.

Some homes do not have a money shortage; they have a stability shortage.

The Altar of Appearance rules and encourages poverty. Looking wealthy while privately collapsing. Image over substance. Luxury before foundation. Emotional spending. Status purchases. Performance prosperity. Need to appear successful.

Some people sacrifice financial peace to maintain visual identity.

The obvious **Altar of Fear & Scarcity.** Constant fear: "We'll never have enough." panic spending, hoarding, inability to build, inability to invest, inability to rest, chronic anxiety around provision. Children raised in this atmosphere often inherit financial fear as identity.

The Altar of Consumption Without Production will tend to poverty and serve as a money blocker. Endless entertainment. No building. No learning. No creating. No developing. No planting. No discipline. Only consuming. Hours, days, weeks, months, and years disappear daily while nothing grows.

A house that consumes constantly but produces little eventually weakens itself. There's a cursed spoon in your cabinet? -- I'm not saying there's not… you'd better check that because I believe objects can be cursed or can be a hindrance to productivity, progress, and life. Else, charms, *mauthes*, (sp), witchcraft would never work, especially against money and progress.

MOVE!

Ever notice that when you are in a hurry, the slowest vehicle somehow finds its way directly in front of you? You are focused, moving, trying to get somewhere, and suddenly momentum changes. Traffic slows. Somebody drifts into your lane. Somebody starts wandering in the aisle at the exact moment you are trying to pass through. Suddenly the phone rings. Suddenly confusion erupts. Suddenly somebody urgently "needs" you. Suddenly unnecessary drama materializes right before progress. Many people have experienced these moments so often that they stop recognizing them as interruption at all; they normalize them.

Blockers often control pace. They force unwanted timing. They create frustration, bottlenecks, delays, interruptions, and emotional exhaustion. One of the most dangerous effects of long-term obstruction is adaptation. Some people have been blocked so long that they no longer recognize blockage as abnormal. Delay becomes identity. Frustration becomes personality. Confusion becomes atmosphere. They stop expecting movement because interruption has become familiar.

This is why recognition alone is not enough. Some people recognize blockers, study blockers, discuss blockers, discern blockers, pray about blockers, analyze blockers, and still never move. At some point discernment must produce action. Wisdom is not merely the ability to identify what is wrong. Wisdom eventually demands movement.

Scripture repeatedly reveals how important movement is in the life of faith. Abram had to leave his father's house. Lot had to leave Sodom. Israel had to leave Egypt. Ruth had to leave Moab. Elijah was told to go to Zarephath. Joseph had to move into Egypt. The disciples left their nets. The man at Bethesda was eventually told to rise. Israel repeatedly had to move the camp, cross rivers, go forward, continue journeying. Movement matters because environments shape people. Remaining too long in the wrong environment eventually reshapes identity itself.

Psychologically, many people stay too long. They remain in dead relationships that loop emotionally and endlessly. They remain in draining systems, warfare zones, manipulative environments, chronic confusion, and cycles that consume Peace and momentum. Worse, some people remain in places where Ichabod has already been written over the door. The glory has departed. The grace for that season is gone; the Peace is gone. Yet people continue clinging emotionally to places, relationships, systems, and identities that God has already exited.

Some people keep praying for change while refusing movement. They pray for Peace while remaining inside chaos. They pray for healing while remaining attached to what continues wounding them. They pray for open doors while refusing to leave dead environments. They pray for clarity while remaining emotionally entangled with confusion. Sometimes the blocker is not what is chasing you. Sometimes the blocker is your refusal to leave.

This is why mature discernment understands that not every battle should be fought head-on. Some people remain emotionally trapped because they believe leaving means failure. Others remain because they crave vindication. Others stay because they fear the unknown. Others continue forcing passage through blocked systems because they mistake stubbornness for faithfulness. But many breakthroughs begin not with confrontation, but with movement.

There are seasons where wisdom reroutes rather than fights. There are seasons where movement means strategic silence instead of public explanation. There are seasons where movement means ending agreements, changing environments, establishing boundaries, practicing discipline, removing access, confronting unhealthy cycles, or walking away from relationships and systems that continuously consume clarity, Peace, and momentum.

Movement requires courage because blockers rarely leave quietly. Some people resist your movement because your movement changes the relationship. Others resist because your movement exposes their stagnation. Others resist because your movement removes access they once enjoyed. Some systems survive specifically because everyone inside them remains emotionally stationary.

Thresholds are uncomfortable because crossing them requires leaving something behind. Israel could not remain emotionally tied to Egypt while inheriting promise. Lot could not linger comfortably in Sodom while judgment approached. Ruth could not remain in Moab while stepping into redemption history. Abram could not become Abraham without movement. The man at Bethesda eventually had to stop merely discussing his condition and rise.

There are seasons where discernment is no longer enough. Movement becomes necessary. Some movement is external, some is internal. Some people physically left years ago while remaining emotionally trapped in the same place. Others remain physically present while internally refusing growth, healing, obedience, maturity, or change. But God continually calls people forward. Forward through wilderness, fear, rebuilding, uncertainty, obedience, grief, healing, and transition.

This is why Jesus spoke about speaking to mountains. Some barriers must be addressed directly. Some obstacles must be commanded to move. Sometimes the blockade itself must be confronted spiritually, emotionally, mentally, or practically. Speak to the mountain. Speak to the barrier. Speak to the obstacle. Speak to the blocker: Move.

In the Name of Jesus. Amen.

PLAYING CHESS, IN THE SPIRIT

Obstacles, blockers... think of a chess board. you don't need to know how to play chess, except in the spirit. Blockers are not just random frustrations, they become strategic interference.

You don't need to know how to play chess… except in the spirit. If you're walking along in life thinking that what you see with your natural eyes is all there is, you'd better think again. Discernment matters; what's going on spiritually around you? Positioning matters; where are you in the scheme of things. Are there enemies nearby? Is the Presence of God something you can sense? Do you have spiritual protection? Have you agreed with God that the Angels of God are near to protect you, to keep you in all your ways?

Movement matters. Do you go left or right today, or do you continue straight ahead? Has the Lord ordered your steps and lit your path and are you walking in the way He said to walk? Moves shouldn't be emotional; they should be ordered.

Some attacks are direct, some are indirect. Some are in your face; others are occult. What is your dream state like?

Some doors and openings are traps. Some blockers are bait. Ooh that looks good, but is it. I keep getting offers from some place where I never applied. They say they can fund me a million dollars. What would I need that for? Who are these people? How much does this cost? No way. I call that, 'trying to sell me money'. Money is earned, it is received, but is money purchased and sold? I don't think so. Jesus turned the moneychangers' table over in the sanctuary, so as far as I'm concerned, it is overturned in the world, at least as it pertains to me.

In chess, pieces block pathways. Lanes are opened up or movement is restricted. Territory matters in chess, in the natural and in the spirit as well.

Advancement in the game, on the board, and in life requires awareness. one wrong move can change many things, or everything; it can set off a cascade of events. In chess, sometimes you are trapped slowly, not suddenly. It's almost like you are watching it in real time or in slow motion, but can you do anything about it?

In Christ, yes. Stay vigilant. Stay prayed up. Walk wisely. Stay in your right position and don't take your eyes off the board. This is what blockers are really good at, distraction--, well, it's the devil's number one strategy. He can do it through eye candy, emotional bait, appealing to greed and lust that shouldn't even be in you in the first place. He will even do this at church. There are sacrificial traps, false openings. Even at church if GOD didn't say tell all your business to the congregation or to your neighbor, then don't. "Turn and tell your neighbor..." Tell your neighbor what*? I won't.*

Hannah was praying like a maniac, but nobody could hear what she was praying – but God. And that time, did

Penninah block her? Nope. Hannah went on to have several more children after Samuel.

Strategic delays are strategized because the enemy has information on your plans and planned moves. QUIET. Protect your plans. Protect valuable pieces. Do not overextend or expose yourself unnecessarily.

Focus when you must but do not get trapped by tunnel vision… know what's going on around you in the natural and in the spirit. Some people lose because they only see the move in front of them. A blocker is not always meant to stop you permanently. Sometimes it is trying to force a bad move.

A lot of witch moves are to do one bad thing that sends a person spiraling, so they do the rest of the damage to themselves, themselves. Pray God, that is never you, in the Name of Jesus.

The Bible is full of strategic positioning.

Why?

Because we need it. Because we are in warfare or at least trying to avoid warfare on a daily basis. It's like driving a car you are constantly looking out for the other vehicles and watching their moves.

We need to be aware because the enemy is wily. There are ambushes, gates, watchmen watching, and strongmen guarding places that we should have access to. There are traps and snares set at noonday, in the night, anytime, really. If the enemy could encompass you about, he would. There are narrow paths, diversions, walls, and sieges.

Timing is of the ultimate importance. You need to know where YOU are, in both space and TIME and what is around you at all times. Blockers are not only about *what* is blocking you, they are also about where you are, *when* you are, what season you are in, what surrounds you, what has access to you, as well as, what is influencing movement around you. That's strategic awareness.

Know the season they're in. Recognize transitions. Understand positioning. Notice environmental influence. Recognize who has proximity. Understand timing, and recognize traps before you're inside the trap.

Some people are fighting the wrong thing because they do not understand where they are on the board. Timing changes everything. The same move that works in one season may destroy you in another.

Issachar understood times and seasons. Everyone is not Issachar or from that tribe, but by the Holy Spirit you can know where you are supposed to be and when.

Watchmen on walls watch for our souls. We need to discern the true watchman before there is a problem and learn how to hear from the Holy Spirit as well as the man of God that the Lord puts in place.

If the Hebrews coming out of Egypt had understood timing, do you think they would have spent all that time wandering? No, they would have understood wilderness transitions and flowed right into the Promised Land.

Jesus recognized time and timing. Amen. He said "my hour has not yet come"

The issue is not only what is blocking you. The issue is whether you understand where **<u>you</u>** are standing. **<u>You must understand the board and timing.</u>** Else, the enemy will make you random offers all the time that are really temptations.

After a while, I realized blockers were not random. Position mattered. Timing mattered. Access mattered. Movement mattered. Environment mattered. Awareness mattered. Suddenly life no longer looked like chaos; it looked like positioning.

STUMBLING BLOCKS

Stumbling blocks are things placed in the path that can mislead, delay, entangle, distract, hook emotionally, confuse discernment, or shift someone gradually out of alignment. They are not necessarily prisons, or catastrophic destruction. But Stumbling blocks are often effective precisely because they do *not* initially appear dangerous.

They often appear pleasant, reasonable, beautiful, friendly, comforting, normal, or beneficial. What can look normal from a distance may not look good upon a more discerning look. Closer inspection revealed something off underneath it. That is almost a textbook symbolic picture of discernment around stumbling blocks seeing beyond presentation into environment/source/foundation.

A friendly atmosphere can conceal another intention entirely. That is also stumbling-block territory: false relational positioning. Stumbling blocks are not always overt evil; sometimes they are misaligned access points.

Once people normalize what feels "slightly off," they can begin adapting themselves around the obstruction instead of recognizing it. Some obstacles are not there merely to stop movement; some are there to alter direction, or alter judgment, appetite, or alignment. The subtlety matters. Because a person rarely says, "I want deception." But they may say, "It's probably fine." "Maybe I'm overthinking." "They seem nice." "It looks good enough." "At least it's something." "It's not that serious."

Over time those small accommodations can produce very large consequences. You must notice any disparity, notice the mismatch before participation.

Are blockers are sent as a first line, or could that be all the enemy is allowed to place in a Believer's life? Or do we know? Scripture does not really present a neat universal hierarchy like "First blockers, then worse things." Life and spiritual opposition seem more layered and situational than that.

Not every form of opposition looks like catastrophe from the onset; some if masked. Sometimes resistance appears as delay, confusion, entanglement. repeated interruption, misdirection, exhaustion, relational complications, temptation, appetite manipulation. atmosphere disruption, loss of focus, destabilization. In other words, many "blockers" function more subtly than dramatic destruction.

Honestly, subtle obstruction is often more effective because people cooperate with it unknowingly. A person notices obvious danger. They may not notice chronic distraction, constant derailment, wrong alignments, draining relationships, cycles of *almost*, or continual low-grade confusion.

Different believers experience very different levels of warfare, pressure, temptation, opposition, consequences, testing, and suffering. Scripture shows Believers encountering temptation, persecution, deception attempts, oppression, betrayal, affliction, weariness, spiritual resistance, strongholds, persecution from systems and people.

Sometimes the enemy does not need total destruction. Simple obstruction may accomplish enough, keep the person distracted, unstable, emotionally reactive, out of position, misaligned, or perpetually delayed. That alone can prevent clarity, Peace, focus, fruitfulness, healing, or forward movement. Not every obstruction is a wall. Some are invitations.

"You cannot move," is far different than, "Move over here instead." That is often harder to detect. A stumbling block can become spiritually and psychologically dangerous when people focus only on the object while ignoring the structure behind it or anything unseen that may be perched on it.

A person may see the delay, the confusion, the draining relationship, the recurring interruption, the pattern of almost, the strange resistance, the emotional heaviness, the repeated derailment— but fail to ask, "What is attached to this?" "What is this sitting over?" "What invisible thing keeps feeding this?" "What is this connected to?"

Sometimes the visible obstruction is merely the perch. The unseen part is the tether, or the handler. It could be the conditioning, or the atmosphere. It could be the agreement, or the appetite being manipulated. It could be the false identity formed around the limitation.

Many people spend years attacking visible symptoms while remaining completely connected to the invisible structure producing them.

A person may remove one "block" and encounter another if the deeper system was never addressed. If there is a chain of blocks or a network, that must be discerned. That is why discernment matters beyond reaction.

So, we don't just ask, "What is happening?" But: "What is operating here?" "What remains unseen?" "What benefits from my stagnation?" "What keeps trying to redirect my movement?" "What keeps presenting itself as normal when something underneath feels wrong?"

One of the most dangerous unseen things attached to a block is adaptation. When a person begins building their identity around obstruction, the block no longer needs force to remain effective. The person starts organizing life around limitation, lower expectations, smaller movement, reduced vision, careful hope, managed desire, emotional self-protection, avoidance of risk, fear of disappointment. At that point, the unseen structure has become internalized.

This brings us back to the perch: eventually the bird returns on its own. That may be one of the deepest forms of blockage there is; a captive with wings and an open sky, but it returns to the perch and just sits there. It's blocked.

SPIRITUAL BLOCKERS

Spiritual blockers are different. Some are in the waking life; they are *sent*. Some are in the dream life, they are sent too. We must always discern the source, who sent them.

False people/things/fruit etc are presented as blockers. These are things of distraction, contamination, delay, entanglement, or momentum disruption rather than outright destruction. Misaligned offerings, false alignment, wrong attachments, or subtle diversions entering relational/emotional space.

Sometimes blockage is not a wall, a demon behind a tree, or obvious opposition. Sometimes it is a blocker system.

Sometimes the blockage is the wrong connection, the wrong atmosphere, the wrong invitation, the wrong emotional entanglement, the wrong "fruit," the wrong agreement. Things that consume attention, drain Peace, complicate movement, muddy discernment, or pull a person sideways. Presentation without authenticity. Friendly wasn't truly friendly. Fruit wasn't rooted in healthy ground. Natural-looking things were positioned over something artificial. That's very blocker-system language.

Blocker systems often work through confusion, misdirection, emotional hooks, false comfort, disguised agendas, synthetic nourishment, relational intrusion, atmosphere disruption.

So, once a person steps out of alignment and makes wrong steps that is the unintended foray into error. Often the drift into error is much quieter and more incremental than people imagine.

Usually it is not, "Today I choose destruction." It is more like, misread friendliness, lowered discernment, ignored discomfort, rationalized compromise, wrong attachment, continued exposure, small agreements, emotional overrides, or staying connected to something that already felt "off." That's why discernment matters so much *before* full entanglement.

Many wrong paths begin looking harmless, social, comforting, reasonable, flattering, helpful, or "natural."

In real life, people often evaluate only the visible fruit. *OH, that looks good. I want that. That looks like a good opportunity. Oh, they look good... affection, chemistry. Oh, that person sounds good, I like what they are saying, charisma. That person is easy to talk to or access, so I'll go with them.*

Many scammers and Ponzi schemers are easy to access --, well at first. Too many people believe too many promises. So many need relief that they may go with the first thing or person offering the appearance of relief only to find that those are traps.

Discernment asks, “What is this rooted over?” “What atmosphere surrounds this?” “What system is attached to this?” This looks good from a distance, but what happens if I keep moving closer?”

Once someone repeatedly steps outside alignment, they can gradually enter confusion, instability, bondage, distraction, or cycles that were never the intended path. This is not always through rebellion either, sometimes through exhaustion, loneliness, flattery, or fear. Sometimes if is because of desperation, the need for relief, the need to belong, or the need to be seen.

That’s why blocker systems can be subtle. Sometimes the “blocker” is not simply stopping movement. Sometimes it is redirecting movement into unfruitful territory.

Defilement is a blocker. This is both in the natural and in the dream state. Certain dog dreams, for example, indicate the *spirit of lust* is active or has been sent against you. This is for the purpose of defilement. Once defiled, even in the dream, blessings can be easily stolen.

Evil birds eat up blessings of the day, the next day.

Turtles. Any slow creatures in the dream are blockers and hindrances to your progress.

NAVIGATING AROUND THEM

One of the greatest signs of maturity is learning that not every blocker must be confronted head-on. Some people waste enormous amounts of emotional energy fighting battles that wisdom would simply bypass. They exhaust themselves trying to force open closed doors, prove points to resistant people, defeat every critic, expose every manipulator, answer every accusation, or confront every obstruction directly. Eventually their entire life becomes organized around resistance instead of movement.

Wisdom moves differently.

Not every obstruction deserves emotional energy.

This is important because many people imagine strength only in terms of confrontation. They believe maturity means aggressively opposing every difficulty, every blocker, every enemy, every challenge, every disagreement, every delay. But Scripture repeatedly shows something more nuanced. Sometimes God parts the sea. Sometimes He collapses the wall. Sometimes He strengthens people to endure. Sometimes He says wait. And sometimes He simply reroutes the journey entirely.

Israel did not fight every nation immediately. Jesus did not answer every accusation. David fled Saul repeatedly rather than confronting him prematurely. Paul was lowered over a wall in a basket to escape danger rather than standing publicly to prove fearlessness. Even Christ Himself sometimes withdrew quietly from hostile environments because the timing was not yet right.

Mature people learn timing matters.

Not every battle is meant for this moment.

One of the most difficult lessons in life is understanding that movement and confrontation are not always the same thing. Some people become so fixated on defeating blockers that they stop progressing altogether. They remain emotionally chained to the obstruction because their entire focus becomes proving, fighting, exposing, arguing, defending, correcting, or resisting.

Sometimes Wisdom simply takes another route.

This is not cowardice. This is strategy.

There are moments when a closed door is not an invitation to break it down. Sometimes the closed door itself is information. Not every inaccessible thing is meant to be pursued indefinitely. Some people remain emotionally trapped for years trying to force movement in places where Grace, Peace, favor, clarity, or timing no longer exist.

Recognizing closed doors is a form of discernment.

This is difficult because human pride often interprets rerouting as defeat. People want validation. They want victory. They want resolution. They want the blocker removed publicly and dramatically. But many times wisdom quietly redirects movement elsewhere. A mature person eventually learns not to confuse persistence with stubbornness.

There is a difference between perseverance and emotional fixation.

Some people are not blocked because the way is impossible. They are blocked because they refuse alternate routes.

This is where strategic silence becomes important. Not every plan should be announced prematurely. Not every vision requires immediate exposure. Not every opportunity should be discussed publicly while still developing. Some movement survives specifically because it remains quiet long enough to mature without unnecessary interference.

Jesus repeatedly instructed people not to broadcast certain things immediately. Nehemiah rebuilt while opposition surrounded him. Wisdom understands that visibility attracts resistance. Some people announce movement too early and then become emotionally entangled in defending what should have been developed efficiently, without fanfare.

There are seasons where silence protects momentum.

Not secrecy born from fear, but restraint born from Wisdom.

Working quietly is deeply underrated in modern culture because many people feel pressured to constantly display progress, announce plans, perform visibility, seek validation, or prove movement publicly. But quiet movement is often protected movement. A seed develops underground long before visible growth appears above the surface.

Some things survive because they grow privately first.

Rerouting energy is another form of Wisdom many people never learn. Some blockers remain powerful simply because too much energy continues flowing toward them. Emotional energy. Mental energy. Conversational energy. Financial energy. Spiritual energy. Attention itself becomes fuel. A person can unknowingly strengthen blockage by obsessing over it constantly.

What continually receives focus often gains power psychologically.

This is why some people begin healing only after they stop centering their lives around the obstruction. They stop replaying old battles endlessly. They stop mentally arguing with absent people. They stop organizing every decision around resistance. They stop feeding emotional cycles that consume momentum. Eventually energy begins flowing back toward building, healing, creating, learning, resting, growing, and moving again.

Every battle does not deserve lifelong occupancy, and free rent in the mind.

Patience also requires maturity because patience is not stagnation. Many people confuse the two. Passive people call stagnation patience. Fearful people call avoidance patience. Emotionally exhausted people sometimes stop moving entirely and label it waiting on God. Biblical patience is active trust. It continues preparing. Continues building. Continues learning, continues positioning, maturing, and observing timing wisely without surrendering movement internally.

Patience without movement becomes paralysis. Movement without Wisdom becomes recklessness. Mature people eventually learn how to remain at Peace during delay without emotionally collapsing into bitterness, panic, or despair. This is another reason Wisdom matters more than aggression alone. Some people know how to fight, but they do not know how to move strategically. They become emotionally inflamed every time resistance appears. Everything becomes personal. Everything becomes war. Everything becomes confrontation.

But Wisdom asks different questions. Is this worth fighting directly? Is this the right timing? Is this really obstruction, or redirection? Is this battle productive, or merely consuming energy?

Would Peace increase more through confrontation or through rerouting? Some of the greatest movement in life occurs after people stop trying to force passage through places that no longer align with Peace, clarity, purpose, or Grace. Sometimes Wisdom is rerouting without bitterness.

Many people reroute physically while remaining emotionally trapped in resentment. They leave environments but carry the offense. They leave relationships but carry the warfare mentally. They move locations while dragging old battles into new seasons. True navigation requires emotional release as well as directional change.

A mature person eventually understands that freedom is not always defeating every blocker dramatically. Sometimes freedom is simply no longer being emotionally controlled by the obstruction at all.

That is Wisdom.

Many people begin moving again the moment they realize they do not have to spend their entire lives standing in front of the same wall demanding it become a door.

Navigate around them when direct removal isn't possible. The blocker isn't removable yet. The system won't change; the person won't change; the season won't change, then Wisdom becomes navigation.

That is LIFE. Not every blocker requires the same response. Because life maturity is learning the difference between confrontation, removal, endurance, adaptation, rerouting, abandonment, patience, warfare, and Wisdom.

Biblically this is everywhere. God did this Himself. Sometimes He removed the blocker. Other times, He parted the blocker, destroyed the blocker, outlasted the blocker, and rerouted around the blocker. God sometimes strengthened people within the blocker or used the blocker itself.

The barrier that is the Jericho wall was completely destroyed.

The Red Sea was completely parted.

The Wilderness was navigated through.

Paul endured the thorn in his side.

Joseph survived the pit. He endured the slavery. He escaped Potiphar's wife. He endured the prison as he survived within it.

David avoided direct confrontation with Saul.

Tamar outplayed Judah.

Rahab outplayed the spies.

Jesus slipped through crowds, strategically.

Nehemiah rebuilt despite opposition; he worked around the blockers.

Immaturity responds to every blocker the same way. Wisdom discerns the correct response.

Some things must be confronted. Some things must be bypassed. Some things must simply be outlasted.

REMOVE THE BLOCKER

Satan, get thee behind me. How do we get the blocker from obstructing both our view and our passage and progress?

At some point, recognition is no longer enough.

There comes a moment in life when a person must stop only identifying blockers and begin removing them. Discernment matters. Awareness matters. Understanding patterns matters. But recognition without action eventually becomes another form of stagnation. A person can spend years explaining why movement is difficult while never confronting the thing obstructing movement itself.

Eventually the blocker must move.

One of the most powerful statements Jesus ever made concerning obstruction was simple and direct: "Satan, get thee behind me." The statement reveals something profound about blockers. Some things are standing in the wrong position. They obstruct vision because they stand in front of the person instead of behind them. They obstruct movement because they occupy pathways they were never meant to occupy.

A blocker standing in front of you affects more than movement. It affects sight.

This is why unresolved obstruction often produces confusion. When something is standing improperly in your path, your perspective becomes distorted. You begin reacting emotionally instead of wisely. You begin making decisions based on fear, exhaustion, frustration, insecurity, or delay. Your vision narrows. Your peace weakens. Your clarity becomes unstable. The blocker occupies so much emotional and psychological space that eventually it dominates thought itself.

Some people are not merely blocked externally. Their entire field of vision has become blocked.

This is why removing blockers is not merely about progress. It is about clarity.

Many people cannot see properly because unresolved obstruction has consumed their focus for too long. They think about the blocker constantly. They react to the blocker constantly. They organize their lives around the blocker. Their emotions revolve around the blocker. Their identity becomes entangled with the blocker. Eventually the obstruction becomes larger in their minds than movement itself.

This is one reason Jesus responded so sharply in moments where obstruction threatened assignment, clarity, timing, or obedience. "Get behind me" was not merely rejection. It was repositioning. Some things must be moved out of leadership position in a person's life. Some voices must be moved behind rather than followed. Some fears must be moved behind. Some relationships, emotional attachments, and wounds must be set behind you. Some distractions must be moved behind. Some systems must lose access to the front of your life.

Not everything deserves front-row positioning.

This chapter is not about aggression for its own sake. It is about rightful positioning. Some blockers remain powerful simply because they have been granted centrality they were never meant to have. Fear sits at the front. Trauma sits at the front. insecurity sits at the front. Emotional dependency sits at the front. Bitterness sits at the front. Chaos sits at the front. Certain people sit at the front. Their influence determines movement, timing, emotions, and decisions.

Eventually wisdom says: move.

Some blockers are removed spiritually. Others relationally, some emotionally. Some require prayer. Others require boundaries. Repentance and disciplines of the faith will rid you of some. Others require difficult conversations, ending access and setting boundaries. Some require changing environments. Some blockers leave quickly once recognized. Others resist removal because they have occupied territory for years.

This is why many people delay removal. Removal is uncomfortable.

Removing blockers often means grieving what should never have occupied such a central place in the first place. It means accepting uncomfortable truths. It means admitting that certain patterns are destructive. It means acknowledging that some relationships harm more than help. It means confronting emotional dependence. It means dismantling agreements that once felt safe. It means releasing identities built around pain, delay, fear, or dysfunction.

Unresolved blockers rarely become harmless through neglect. What remains in the path continues obstructing movement. This is why partial obedience often produces continued frustration. A person removes symptoms while protecting the root. They pray for peace while feeding chaos. They ask for movement while maintaining entanglement. They seek clarity while refusing honesty. They ask God to open doors while repeatedly rebuilding the same obstruction in front of the doorway.

Some blockers survive because people secretly prefer familiar obstruction over unfamiliar freedom. Freedom changes responsibility. Movement changes identity. Progress changes expectations. Once the blocker moves, the person must eventually move too. This is why removal requires courage.

Sometimes the blocker is external. Sometimes it is internalized, or inherited, relational, emotional. Sometimes it is spiritual. Sometimes the blocker is not a demon, enemy, or attacker at all. Sometimes the blocker is the version of yourself that became comfortable living beneath your true capacity.

Many people keep praying for God to remove things He is waiting for them to confront.

David still had to approach Goliath. Israel still had to step toward the Jordan. The people still had to walk around Jericho. The stone still had to be acknowledged before it could be moved. Even miracles often required movement, participation, obedience, or confrontation from those involved.

This is important because some people imagine blocker removal as entirely passive. They wait endlessly for circumstances to change while refusing every difficult decision that would create movement. But many blockers remain powerful because nobody has yet decided that enough is enough.

Eventually there comes a moment when the exhaustion of remaining blocked becomes greater than the discomfort of change. That moment matters.

Because once the blocker moves, sight changes. Breathing changes. Thinking changes. Energy changes. Movement changes. Peace changes. Possibility returns. Momentum, and clarity return. A person who has lived obstructed for years often does not even realize how much energy blockage consumed until the obstruction is finally removed.

Some people have spent so long staring at blockers that they forgot movement was possible.

God never intended for human beings to spend their entire lives trapped behind what should have been moved long ago. Sometimes the most spiritual thing a person can say is simple, direct, and long overdue: **Move**.

REMOVE THE BLOCK (THE BLOCKADE)

And a stone of stumbling, and a rock of offence, even to them which stumble at the word, being disobedient: whereunto also they were appointed. (1 Peter 2:8)

And he shall be for a sanctuary; but for a stone of stumbling and for a rock of offence to both the houses of Israel, for a gin and a snare to the inhabitants of Jerusalem. (Isaiah 8:14)

A blockade is different from a blocker. A blocker may be a person, a *spirit*, a relationship, a mindset, a gatekeeper, or a single point of obstruction. A blockade is broader. A blockade is sustained obstruction. It is a surrounding system that restricts movement, drains resources, interrupts access, and slowly wears down strength over time. Historically, a blockade was a military strategy designed to isolate a city or nation by cutting off access, movement, supply lines, communication, escape routes, provisions, and reinforcement. The goal was not always direct destruction. Often the goal was exhaustion. Hunger. Weakening. Psychological collapse. Surrender through prolonged restriction, a siege, rather than immediate attack.

Many folks remove individual blockers while failing to recognize the blockade itself remains intact. Removing one manipulative person does not automatically remove the emotional atmosphere they created. Ending a toxic relationship does not automatically dismantle the soul-level obstruction left behind. Firing one corrupt leader does not instantly heal a dysfunctional culture. Removing one fearful thought does not erase years of fear-conditioning. Leaving Egypt did not remove the Red Sea. Defeating one enemy does not automatically dismantle an entire system of obstruction.

People become frustrated because they believe movement should immediately return once a visible blocker disappears. But blockades are structural. Environmental. Psychological. Spiritual. Generational. Systemic. They often continue functioning long after the original source appears gone.

This is why some people are no longer blocked externally yet still live internally barricaded. Trauma, fear, emotional scars, learned helplessness can all be blockades. Hypervigilance after prolonged chaos can become a blockade. Betrayal can create an inability to trust that quietly obstructs future relationships for years. Internalized limitations can continue controlling movement long after the original environment changed.

A person may physically leave bondage while mentally remaining surrounded by it.

Israel left Egypt physically long before Egypt fully left them psychologically. The sea itself still blocked movement even after Pharaoh's pursuit. Jericho was not merely people; it was fortified obstruction. The veil in the temple represented restricted access. The stone over the tomb represented sealed limitation. Generational idolatry created national blockades over entire peoples. Unbelief itself blocked entry into promise.

Blockades are dangerous because they affect more than movement alone. They affect expectation. Over time, people adapt to restriction. They stop believing movement is possible. They begin organizing life around survival instead of freedom. Exhaustion becomes normal. Delay becomes identity. Limitation becomes internalized. Eventually people stop asking how to move forward and begin unconsciously assuming they never will.

Removing the blockade requires more than removing one visible obstacle. It requires dismantling systems, healing patterns, removing agreements, restructuring environments, renewing the mind, reopening access, restoring pathways, rebuilding movement itself, and confronting internalized obstruction. Some people pray for open doors while continuing to protect the very systems that keep those doors inaccessible. Others remove external influences while refusing the inner healing necessary for true freedom.

Sometimes the blocker is gone, but the obstruction remains. Removing one person does not automatically remove the atmosphere they built.

This is especially true in environments shaped by chronic instability, manipulation, fear, control, pride systems, confusion cycles, or emotional exhaustion. Even after visible change occurs, the nervous system may still expect chaos. The mind may still expect sabotage. The emotions may still anticipate danger. The person may continue reacting to old warfare long after the battlefield changed.

This is why true restoration is deeper than simple escape. God does not merely remove enemies. He restores movement. He restores clarity. He restores access. He restores expectation. He restores Peace. The goal is not merely surviving obstruction. The goal is freedom from living as though the blockade still controls the future.

Some people spend years after deliverance still emotionally living inside surrounded territory. They remain guarded, fearful, suspicious, reactive, hesitant, and exhausted because the blockade shaped them internally. The blockade itself must be dismantled. Not only around the person, but *within* them.

Some who believe they are still blocked when in reality they are standing in front of gates that have already opened, carrying fears that no longer have authority, protecting wounds that no longer define them, living behind internal barricades that God never intended to be permanent.

BLOCKING SYSTEMS

When the Obstruction Is Bigger Than One Person

Don't be paranoid, but never assume that every obstruction originates from one isolated individual. Sometimes the issue is not just one person; sometimes the obstruction is systemic. It is cultural, relationally reinforced, emotionally maintained, and spiritually embedded. It is woven into the environment itself.

Some blockers are larger than personalities.

Family systems can become blockers. Entire families can unconsciously organize themselves around dysfunction, fear, silence, control, emotional instability, competition, victimhood, addiction, secrecy, or manipulation. In these environments, movement itself becomes threatening because growth by one person disrupts the emotional balance of the entire system. Healing threatens dysfunction. Clarity threatens confusion. Boundaries threaten control. Success threatens comparison. Peace threatens chaos.

This is why some families resist the healthiest person in the room.

The issue is not always hatred. Sometimes systems resist whatever exposes their dysfunction. A person trying to mature inside an immature system often experiences resistance precisely because their movement confronts what others have normalized. In some family systems, everyone unconsciously adapts to the same emotional climate until instability itself becomes identity.

Toxic workplace cultures operate similarly. Some organizations reward exhaustion, manipulation, performance, fear, competition, dishonesty, image management, favoritism, or emotional suppression. People quickly learn what must be sacrificed in order to survive within the system. Over time, healthy movement becomes difficult because the culture itself punishes honesty, balance, clarity, rest, integrity, creativity, or independent thinking.

Some systems survive by exhausting people before they can think clearly enough to leave.

Groupthink is another powerful blocking system. Human beings naturally fear exclusion. Because of this, groups can slowly train individuals to suppress discernment, conscience, Wisdom, intuition, or truth in order to preserve belonging. Entire communities can normalize destructive thinking simply because nobody wants to risk rejection by questioning the system openly.

This is how manipulation networks develop.

In manipulation networks, confusion is often intentionally maintained because confusion weakens resistance. Information becomes distorted. Communication becomes twisted. People become triangulated against each other. Fear spreads quietly. Narratives constantly shift. Loyalty is weaponized. Individuals are emotionally managed through guilt, insecurity, dependency, shame, intimidation, or flattery. The goal is rarely Peace; the goal is control.

This is why some people feel mentally exhausted after spending time inside certain systems. The environment itself drains clarity.

Confusion cycles are one of the clearest signs of a blocking system. Healthy systems eventually produce clarity, stability, accountability, and resolution. Blocking systems produce endless emotional fog. The same conflicts repeat without resolution. The same instability recycles endlessly. Conversations never truly clarify anything. Misunderstandings multiply instead of decreasing. Drama becomes perpetual. Emotional exhaustion becomes normal.

People inside these systems often lose perspective gradually because dysfunction repeated long enough eventually feels ordinary.

Chronic instability also functions as a blocking system. Some people never experience enough Peace, predictability, structure, rest, or emotional stability to build consistently because the environment itself continuously interrupts movement. Crisis replaces rhythm. Emergency replaces planning. Survival replaces growth. The system consumes all available energy simply maintaining itself.

This is one reason some people remain blocked despite talent, intelligence, or desire. Constant instability prevents sustained momentum.

Performance systems are another major source of obstruction. In these systems, image matters more than truth. Presentation matters more than integrity. *Looking* successful matters more than being healthy. Everything becomes performance. Spirituality becomes performance. Relationships become performance. Prosperity becomes performance. Leadership becomes performance. Eventually individuals lose connection with authenticity because survival inside the system depends on maintaining appearances.

Performance systems are exhausting because people can never rest honestly within them. Pride structures strengthen many blocking systems. Pride resists correction, humility, Truth, and accountability.. Some systems become impossible to heal because everyone inside them is more committed to preserving image than confronting reality. In pride structures, Truth becomes threatening because Truth destabilizes illusion. This is where Leviathan becomes evident.

Most people hear the word Leviathan and think only of a sea serpent or mythical creature. Biblically and spiritually, Leviathan represents far more than imagery of a creature in water. Leviathan represents twisting, distortion, pride, escalation, and confusion. It represents resistance to Peace, Truth, humility and resolution.

Leviathan twists communication. This is one of its clearest characteristics. Conversations, intentions, and words become distorted. Peaceful communication somehow escalates into conflict repeatedly. People begin reacting to distorted interpretations of what was said. Simple disagreements become emotional explosions. Offense multiplies rapidly. Pride hardens quickly. Resolution becomes increasingly difficult because the system itself feeds misunderstanding.

Leviathan thrives where pride prevents humility.

This is why some conflicts never resolve. Nobody can admit wrong. Nobody can soften. Nobody can apologize honestly. Nobody can step back emotionally. Everyone becomes locked into defense, accusation, escalation, and self-protection. The system itself feeds conflict continuously.

This twisting dynamic often appears in families, churches, workplaces, friendships, leadership structures, marriages, organizations, and communities. What began as a simple issue becomes emotionally tangled beyond proportion. People become suspicious. Defensive. Inflamed. Exhausted. Narratives multiply. Communication deteriorates. Truth becomes increasingly difficult to locate beneath emotional distortion. Leviathan also resists Peace itself.

Some environments cannot tolerate Peace for long. Calm feels uncomfortable. Stability feels suspicious. Resolution feels threatening. Something constantly reintroduces conflict, confusion, accusation, drama, tension, or emotional agitation. This is why some people leave certain environments feeling mentally twisted, emotionally inflamed, or spiritually exhausted without fully understanding why the system itself feeds turbulence.

Relational triangulation is one of the clearest manifestations of this dynamic. Instead of direct communication, people communicate through third parties, emotional alliances, gossip, manipulation, passive aggression, secret conversations, and divided loyalties. People are emotionally pulled into conflicts that should have remained direct and simple. Confusion multiplies because clarity is never allowed to remain straightforward.

Leviathan thrives in environments where truth becomes tangled. Spiritual discernment matters deeply. Not every difficult relationship indicates Leviathan. Not every disagreement is spiritual warfare. Human beings are imperfect and conflict naturally occurs. But when twisting, confusion, escalation, pride, emotional turbulence, distortion, and resistance to Peace become chronic patterns across entire systems, Wisdom must recognize that something larger than one isolated disagreement may be operating.

Blocking systems are dangerous because individuals inside them often adapt unconsciously. People normalize confusion, instability, emotional exhaustion, pride, manipulation, tension and chaos. Eventually they stop recognizing how unhealthy the environment really is.

This is why movement sometimes requires more than changing one relationship. Sometimes the entire system must be exited, confronted, restructured, healed, or dismantled.

Some blockers are not standing in one person alone. Some blockers are woven into the atmosphere itself.

DEATH WAS THE LAST BLOCKER

All through the Old Testament we see how Death blocked people. Death blocked Tamar from producing an heir, it blocked all the widows who were left suffering, it blocked Naomi.

Spiritual death blocked Adam and Eve. The cherubim with the flaming sword that turns every which way was one of God's blockers. He blocked Adam and Eve from returning to the Garden of Eden. the Red Sea blocked the Hebrews from leaving Egypt until God sent a work around. Same for the the Jericho Wall, and the Jordan, until Joshua did what God said to do.

Sin blocked the priest who went in once a year to minister in the Holy of Holies who had a rope tied about his leg so if he died, he could be dragged out.

A man's own mind can be a blocker. This is why we must cast down imaginations. Think on *these things*, according to the Word of God. Wrong words are not words of life; they are words of death.

There is a Biblical pattern of blocked access, blocked inheritance, blocked movement, blocked covenant, blocked promise, blocked progression. Death was a blocker; it blocked entry, lives, and destinies. Death becomes one of the ultimate blockers in Scripture. Not just physical death, but the interruption of continuity, inheritance, fruitfulness, covenant progression, lineage, provision, movement.

Death blocked lineage when Tamar's husband Er, died. Then Onan. Without an heir (male) a woman was to live forever like a widow if her husband died, even if he died very young. Inheritance would be blocked, discontinuation of covenant. This created vulnerability and uncertainty for that woman in that culture.

Naomi looked at widowhood, loss, emptiness and future obstruction. She even tried to change her own name, saying, "Call me Mara"

The cherubim at Eden may become one of the most important "blocker" images in the whole Bible, again confirming that God has blockers too--, well, first. The devil is a copycat. Humanity was blocked from a return to the Garden of Eden because God didn't want man to live forever in that fallen state. The Bible does not say He didn't want man to live forever, just not in the condition of being spiritually dead.

By that block, access was denied, reentry was prevented by the cherubim with the flaming sword guarding the way.

God not only had other blockers, He could speak to any of Creation to become a blocker, just at His Word. He's God like that. The Red Sea was an environmental blocker. God can even take a man-made structure and turn its use to His own use. He is God, *like that.*

Jericho was a structural blocker, but when God takes a thing down, it will stay down unless He says otherwise.

- Jordan = transitional blocker
- Wilderness = progression blocker
- Goliath = fear/intimidation blocker
- Pharaoh = systemic blocker
- Sin = relational blocker between God and man
- Mindset = internal blocker
- Unbelief = inheritance blocker

Then Christ becomes the remover of the ultimate blockage. Jesus consistently moves blockers such as sickness, demons, exclusion, shame, blindness, separation, sin, and Death itself. Jesus defeated Death. Are not all those other things, sickness, demons, poverty, exclusion, etcetera smaller ***expressions*** of Death?

If Jesus took the entire blanket of Death off of mankind then anything squirming beneath because of the Light that it is now exposed to, must also die.

Many of those things can be understood as manifestations, extensions, or operating expressions of death, both physical death, and any separation from the fullness of God's life, order, wholeness, and communion.

The Bible presents "death" as more than a corpse. Death shows up as decay, corruption, bondage, loss, isolation, barrenness, uncleanness, futility, oppression, captivity, fear, destruction, diminishing, poverty, disorder, and ultimately, disconnection from life. Sickness can be viewed as a movement toward Death. Poverty can become a form of diminishment and erosion. Exclusion can reflect separation and alienation. Certain demonic operations produce destruction, fragmentation, torment, and anti-life conditions. Chaos behaves as an anti-life force.

Christ did not just preach forgiveness in abstraction. He healed sickness, cast out demons, and raised the dead. He fed people and restored them to community. Jesus cleansed lepers, opened eyes, restored minds, broke oppression and released captives, confronting Death in its various forms. Christ consistently brings life, light, restoration, increase, Peace, reconciliation, and incorruption. Some conditions feel spiritually "death-like" even when a person is still biologically alive. A person can be emotionally dead, spiritually dead, relationally dead, morally dead, socially cut off, or internally decaying, while still physically breathing.

Biblically, resurrection is often bigger than bodies coming out of graves. It is restoration of life where death had spread. That is why deliverance is freedom; it is, healing, provision, reconciliation, cleansing and wholeness.

Triumphing over Death, at the resurrection, the stone is moved. That blocker is removed for man's eyes; the stone wouldn't have held Jesus anyway. Hell didn't, the grave couldn't. Access to God is restored (Hebrews) from the threat of the heat of Hell, we can approach God again; the veil is torn. The cool of the day is returned, if we will but access it through Jesus Christ. The Good Shepherd shows His greatness as He shepherds mankind out of Hell into green pastures again. Amen. The way reopened. Access is restored.

PRAYER POINTS TO REMOVE BLOCKS

Let the Angels of the living God roll away every stone blocking my financial, physical, emotional, and spiritual breakthroughs, in the Name of Jesus.

Every cloud blocking light, clarity, direction, revelation, and understanding over my life, scatter now, in the Name of Jesus.

Father, demolish every stumbling block placed deliberately or unknowingly in my path, in the Name of Jesus.

Every block hiding my breakthrough, delaying manifestation, or obstructing access, be removed by the power of God, in Jesus' Name.

Every force blocking vision, discernment, Wisdom, strategy, and spiritual sight, loose and lose your hold now, in the Name of Jesus.

Every *spirit of confusion* blocking clarity, focus, timing, Peace, and decision-making, depart from me now, in Jesus' Name.

Every internal barricade built through fear, trauma, unbelief, bitterness, shame, or discouragement, break apart now by the power of God, in the Name of Jesus.

Every gatekeeper standing in opposition to what God has ordained for my life, be moved out of the way according to the will of God, in Jesus' Name.

Every evil blockade surrounding my progress, my family, my calling, my health, my provision, or my movement, be dismantled now, in the Name of Jesus.

Every voice speaking limitation, stagnation, delay, defeat, or impossibility over my life, be silenced, in the Name of Jesus.

Lord, expose every hidden obstruction, every disguised blocker, every sabotaging influence, and every wrong agreement operating against my movement, in Jesus' Name.

Father, restore movement where there has been stagnation, restore clarity where there has been confusion, restore access where there has been blockage, and lead me forward in Wisdom, Peace, obedience, and victory, in the Name of Jesus.

WHO ARE YOU BLOCKING?

It is easy to read a book like this and keep looking outward. Who blocked me? Who delayed me? Who wasted my years? Who interfered with my healing, my progress, my peace, my opportunity, my future? Those are important questions, and some people have experienced real obstruction. But spiritual maturity eventually turns the mirror around. At some point every serious Believer must ask a harder question: what if I am blocking something God intended to flow?

Some people believe they are protecting themselves when they are actually resisting the very thing God sent to help them. Others call correction warfare, accountability hatred, boundaries jealousy, consequences attacks, timing delay, and oppression. Meanwhile, they themselves may be blocking reconciliation, healing, obedience, growth, maturity, responsibility, Truth, provision, opportunity, or Peace. If you are blocking anything other than what God would block, you had better check yourself before you wreck yourself.

That is strong language, but it is necessary because people can become unauthorized gatekeepers without ever admitting it. They stand in thresholds they were never assigned to guard. They use their opinions to control what should be prayed through. Or, they pray amiss.

Some people pray prayers God never authorized because the prayer is rooted in fear, control, jealousy, possession, insecurity, resentment, emotional dependency, competition, or selfish desire rather than the will of God. Not every spiritual-sounding prayer is righteous simply because somebody says "Lord" before it. Human beings can pray soulish prayers that attempt to hold people back, delay movement, preserve unhealthy access, maintain emotional control, block separation, interfere with relationships, frustrate opportunity, or keep others emotionally available for selfish reasons.

Some people pray against marriages because they do not want to lose access to a person emotionally. Others pray against movement because somebody's growth threatens their own comfort, control, or position. Others pray from envy, comparison, offense, wounded pride, or hidden resentment. Some pray for God to "humble" people when what they truly mean is, "Lord, stop them from surpassing me." Others pray for doors to close not because God said no, but because they themselves fear change, loss, distance, irrelevance, exposure, or abandonment.

That is dangerous territory. Especially when you take your soulish desires to the 'prayer team." "Y'all pray for Sister So-And-So, that she won't leave the ministry."

Once selfishness, control, manipulation, envy, emotional dependency, or bitterness enter prayer, the person is no longer interceding purely. They are attempting to spiritually influence outcomes according to their own wounded desires. Some people do this knowingly. Others do it sincerely while remaining completely undiscerning about their own motives. Sincerity does not automatically sanctify selfishness.

They use fear to delay what should be released. They use insecurity to choke what should be celebrated. They use pride to resist correction. They use wounds to justify control. They use emotional pressure, manipulation, guilt, silence, comparison, intimidation, withholding, or confusion to influence outcomes that should belong to God.

Be careful that you do not become the blocker you keep praying against.

Some blocking is painfully ordinary. Please do not become the person who takes over every room, wastes everyone's time, drains emotional bandwidth, consumes attention endlessly, creates unnecessary confusion, or inserts themselves into processes that do not belong to them. Some people block through constant crisis creation. Others through emotional dependency. Others through indecision that traps people in uncertainty for months or years. Others through jealousy, territorial behavior, competition, comparison, manipulation, withholding support, or needing to remain central in situations where they should have stepped aside long ago.

Praying for movement while simultaneously standing in someone else's way is not Wisdom.

Some people are not malicious; they are simply unhealed, immature, insecure, prideful, territorial, emotionally dependent, or unwilling to move themselves. Unresolved people often unconsciously demand that everybody around them stop moving too. They resist growth because someone else's growth exposes their stagnation. They resist change because movement threatens their control. They resist healing because healthy people become harder to manipulate emotionally.

Blockers are often not strangers but people with access. They are close enough to influence Peace, timing, confidence, decisions, momentum, and perception. Sometimes they know too much because too much access was given to them. Sometimes they present as concerned, friendship, support, mentorship, family, or spiritual companionship while quietly consuming momentum through negativity, comparison, fear, distraction, interference, or subtle control. Whether the obstruction is intentional or unintentional, the effect can still be the same. A person can still hinder what God is trying to move.

Scripture repeatedly shows that people can indeed block what God intends. Pharaoh blocked a nation. Saul attempted to block David. Religious systems blocked access while pretending to represent God. Jonah, through rebellion, endangered an entire ship full of innocent people. Unbelief blocked inheritance. Pride blocked Wisdom. Fear blocked movement. Offense blocks reconciliation every day. The pattern is clear: blockers are not always obvious enemies. Often, they are people with proximity, familiarity, influence, access, and emotional entanglement.

This becomes even more dangerous because the world often trains people to become blockers in order to rise.

Many systems reward aggression, domination, manipulation, vanity, image management, self-promotion, exploitation, gatekeeping, emotional coldness, and strategic obstruction. The world teaches people to crush competition, protect image at all costs, stay on top, outshine everybody else, and make sure nobody rises too close beside them. Some people have spent so long functioning inside these systems that obstruction feels normal to them.

But the Kingdom of God teaches a completely different way of living. Blessed are the meek. Blessed are the merciful. Blessed are the peacemakers. Blessed are the pure in heart. The Kingdom teaches service, stewardship, humility, integrity, compassion, justice, Truth, clean hands, and open pathways. Jesus did not teach people to advance by becoming hindrances to others. He taught fruitfulness without corruption, authority without domination, and influence without obstruction.

One of the most dangerous possibilities in life is not that you have been blocked; it is that you have become a blocker yourself.

DON'T MEAN NO HARM

The Blocker Who Means Well

Not every blocker is malicious. Some blockers genuinely believe they are helping. They are not trying to destroy anyone's life, sabotage destiny, or create suffering intentionally. In many cases they are motivated by affection, fear, compassion, protectiveness, emotional attachment, guilt, loyalty, habit, or the sincere desire to prevent pain. Yet good intentions do not automatically produce good outcomes. Some of the greatest delays in human life have not come through hatred, but through misplaced love.

The blocker who *"don't mean no harm"* can wear many faces.

It can be the parent who refuses to let the child mature emotionally because being needed has become part of the parent's identity. Protection slowly becomes control. Guidance slowly becomes interference. The child cannot fully develop because someone is constantly stepping in before growth, responsibility, consequences, or independence can take root. In the beginning this often looks loving. Over time, maturation itself becomes blocked.

I met a 23-year-old college graduate at a luncheon but everything I asked him, his father answered for him. I'm not sure I'd remember the young man's voice at all.

Some parents unintentionally **block** their children by requiring <u>absolutely nothing</u> from them, even well into adulthood. Love without responsibility can quietly produce dependence, passivity, entitlement, emotional immaturity, and delayed development. Human beings often grow through accountability, contribution, effort, discomfort, and learning how to function independently. Some parents remove every obstacle from the child's path, including basic chores, answer every question, solve every problem, absorb every consequence, and carry every burden, then wonder why the child struggles to move confidently through adult life. Love prepares people for life. Control and over-functioning often prepare people for dependence.

A well-intentioned blocker could be the friend who talks someone out of obedience because the path looks too lonely, too uncertain, too difficult, or too costly. Instead of encouraging courage, they encourage comfort. Instead of supporting growth, they reinforce fear. They may sincerely believe they are protecting the person from hardship while unknowingly obstructing movement that God Himself initiated.

It can be the family member who repeatedly reopens doors that needed to remain shut. Every unhealthy cycle receives another opportunity. Every destructive relationship receives another reopening. Every boundary becomes negotiable because someone inside the system cannot tolerate separation, discomfort, confrontation, or change.

What should have ended continues because somebody keeps emotionally resurrecting what Wisdom already buried.

It can be the provider who sustains dysfunction because rescuing others has become emotionally rewarding. Some people feel valuable only when they are needed. Because of this, they unconsciously maintain the weakness, dependency, instability, or immaturity of others. They continually remove consequences before growth can occur. They interrupt processes that might have produced responsibility, discipline, humility, or change.

There is the rescuer, always arriving before anybody has to fully face consequences. There is the interferer, stepping into situations they were never assigned to manage. There is the softener, reducing every serious issue until nobody has to confront reality honestly. There is the overrider, speaking over Wisdom, boundaries, timing, or discernment because their emotions demand immediate relief. There is the comforter who blocks conviction by making every difficult truth feel too harsh to endure.

Then there is the peacekeeper who prevents Truth altogether. This person avoids confrontation in the name of harmony. They smooth over problems that should have been addressed. They silence hard conversations because tension makes them uncomfortable. They protect appearances while deeper rot remains untouched underneath. Outward calm becomes more important than inward honesty. But unresolved truth does not disappear simply because people avoid discussing it. Hidden dysfunction continues growing in silence.

What makes these blockers difficult to recognize is that they are often praised socially. They appear supportive, generous, loyal, nurturing, compassionate, patient, helpful, sacrificial, or kindhearted. Sometimes they genuinely possess many of those qualities. But praise does not change the fruit. If the result is dependence, delay, confusion, emotional paralysis, avoidance, arrested growth, repeated dysfunction, or chronic instability, then something in that "help" has become obstruction instead of blessing.

This is why discernment must evaluate fruit instead of appearances alone. Not all help is healthy. Not all support produces freedom. Not all protection produces growth. Sometimes what appears compassionate externally is actually preventing movement internally.

Scripture reveals this pattern repeatedly. Peter loved Jesus sincerely, yet when he attempted to pull Christ away from the path of sacrifice, Jesus responded sharply because affection itself had become obstruction. Abraham had to leave familiar structures behind in order to move forward. Israel repeatedly struggled with voices longing for Egypt because discomfort in transition made bondage appear emotionally safer than freedom.

Human beings naturally want to relieve discomfort quickly, but discomfort is not always destruction. Sometimes discomfort is process. Sometimes it's refinement. Sometimes it's conviction. Sometimes discomfort is growth. God allows pressure because pressure is exposing what comfort kept hidden.

This is why this book, and specifically this chapter must turn inward before pointing outward. It is not enough only to identify malicious obstruction in others. Every sincere person must ask difficult questions about themselves as well. Has my kindness become control? Has my compassion become interference? Has my loyalty become unhealthy attachment? Has my protection become imprisonment? Has my helping become disobedience?

Those questions require humility because human beings often confuse intention with impact. "I meant well" does not automatically heal the damage caused. A person can sincerely love somebody while still obstructing their growth, maturity, healing, discipline, responsibility, obedience, or movement.

Sometimes the most loving thing a person can do is step back and allow Truth, consequences, process, boundaries, discomfort, or growth to occur without interruption. That requires Wisdom.

If God is using a process to confront, refine, mature, humble, separate, redirect, or transform someone, stepping in outside His Wisdom may not be Mercy at all. It may be blockage wearing the face of care. That means every sincere person eventually must ask the Lord an uncomfortable but necessary question, Am I helping? Or am I standing in the way?

UNBLOCKED.

Some things were never sent to help you progress. They were sent to stand in your way. Some blockers do not stop movement entirely; they stop momentum. That distinction matters because momentum affects nearly everything else in human life. Momentum affects confidence, clarity, focus, discipline, emotional stability, timing, and hope. A person who loses momentum often begins losing expectation as well.

The enemy does not always need to destroy someone completely in order to limit their life. Sometimes delay is enough. Sometimes repeated interruption is enough. Sometimes confusion, distraction, emotional exhaustion, or chronic instability is enough to slowly reduce movement over time. Almost everybody has experienced strange moments where interruption appears at the worst possible time. Noise suddenly appears during rest. Urgency suddenly materializes during breakthrough, prayer, writing, sleep, clarity, Peace, or momentum. A phone that never rings suddenly rings while someone is finally resting or concentrating. The issue is not always the interruption itself. The issue is the pattern. Wisdom notices what consistently breaks concentration, clarity, momentum, Peace, or rest.

At the same time, discernment requires balance. If every interruption becomes “a demon,” people stop thinking clearly. But if a person never notices repeated disruption patterns either, they miss Wisdom entirely. Healthy discernment notices patterns without collapsing into paranoia. This balance matters because many people spend years trying to move forward without recognizing what has consistently stood in their way. Some blockers are external. Some are relational. Some are spiritual. Some are internalized. Some appear through environments, systems, distractions, family dynamics, emotional exhaustion, unhealthy cycles, poor timing, chronic confusion, or repeated misalignment. Over time, people begin honestly examining the patterns operating within their lives. They begin looking at relationships, finances, habits, environments, unfinished goals, delays, emotional fatigue, and recurring cycles that sneakily consume movement and clarity.

One of the most important revelations in this journey is understanding that not all blockers are enemies. Some are warnings. Some are boundaries. Some are consequences. Some are timing mechanisms. Some are Wisdom signals. Some are closed doors functioning as protection rather than punishment. This is what keeps discernment from deteriorating into fear-based thinking where every inconvenience is interpreted as warfare. Human beings often want unrestricted access and unrestricted movement, but unrestricted movement is not always Mercy.

Sometimes restraint itself is Wisdom. Sometimes a closed door prevents destruction. Delay prevents premature movement. Obstruction reveals misalignment rather than attack. Mature discernment learns how to distinguish between destructive obstruction and Divine restraint.

Every blocker cannot be removed directly. Some systems will never cooperate. Some environments will never become healthy. Some people will never understand. Because of this, maturity eventually learns rerouting, timing, strategic silence, conservation of energy, alternate pathways, and preserving Peace.

Do not waste emotional energy trying to force movement through places where Grace, clarity, favor, or timing no longer exist. Wisdom understands that movement and confrontation are not always the same thing. Sometimes movement means leaving. It could mean changing environments, or ending agreements, establishing boundaries, removing access, restructuring life, confronting unhealthy cycles, practicing discipline, or simply refusing to remain emotionally entangled with confusion any longer.

UNBLOCKED. ultimately becomes much deeper than merely defeating enemies. By the end of the journey, unblocked is not simply about warfare. It becomes freedom from bitterness, freedom from obsession, from paranoia, from unnecessary conflict, and freedom from internal obstruction. People who remain chronically blocked often become reactive, defensive, suspicious, frustrated, territorial, emotionally inflamed, and exhausted. They begin expecting conflict everywhere. They start reading enemies into every disagreement and sabotage into every inconvenience. Once movement is restored, once clarity returns, and once the obsession with obstruction finally breaks, something changes internally. A person becomes capable of releasing battles instead of collecting them endlessly. They stop fighting everyone. They stop living in constant resistance. Peace is no longer weakness, appeasement, desperation, or emotional exhaustion. Peace becomes maturity, freedom, stability, confidence, clarity, and spiritual rest.

After an entire journey through obstruction, delay, systems, positioning, entanglement, discernment, navigation, warfare, and timing, **UNBLOCKED** feels earned because it represents restoration rather than mere survival. Spiritually, this is where Christ enters fully as the way maker, the access restorer, the chain breaker, the stone mover, the veil tearer, and resurrection power itself. The moved stone, the torn veil, the reopened path, the fallen wall, the parted river, and the completed crossing all testify to the same truth: some things were never meant to stay blocked forever. God continually restores movement where fear, confusion, delay, bondage, hopelessness, or obstruction once stood. Human beings were never designed to remain trapped indefinitely behind every wall they encounter.

UNBLOCKED is movement restored. Access restored. Perspective restored. It is clarity returning after confusion, Peace returning after warfare, and life returning after prolonged stagnation. It is freedom from living trapped inside endless cycles of frustration, obstruction, and emotional exhaustion. More than anything else, Dear Reader, you now can enjoy forward motion instead of fear.

EPILOGUE

MAKING PEACE WITH YOUR ENEMIES

One of the clearest signs that a person is no longer trapped is the restoration of Peace. There is a profound difference between someone who has become spiritually mature and someone who has become exhausted. Exhausted people sometimes stop fighting because they no longer have energy. Mature people stop fighting unnecessary battles because Wisdom has finally entered the situation.

Now, we do not expect conflict everywhere, but we do look with a discerning eye and we pray and ask the Lord to reveal Truth to us.

Where and whenever it is possible we will endeavor to make peace with our enemies. Or, as the Word says, our enemies will be at peace with us, if it is the Will of God.

When a man's ways please the LORD, he maketh even his enemies to be at peace with him. (Proverbs 16:7)

We do not become blockers, or if we have, we repent and we do not remain as blockers. Spiritual sobriety and self-examination matter so deeply. Scripture does not teach paranoia, constant hostility, imagined warfare against everyone, or endless suspicion. Discernment without Peace eventually becomes suspicion. Some people are fighting battles God never told them to fight.

Human beings are imperfect. Misunderstandings happen. Boundaries happen. Disappointments happen. Honest disagreement happens. If there is a spiritual matter, we take it up spiritually; we do not war against flesh and blood. Take issues into your prayer room and deal with it in the spirit.

As much as lies within you, live peaceably with all men. But if you think they are doing something to you, you can still be civil and deal with it in prayer.

Be sure your ways please God so your enemies will be at Peace with you. Be so aligned with Christ that your enemies won't even want to be enemies with you. Keep yourself upright before God so the enemy has no purchase point into your life.

"Blessed are the peacemakers" does not describe weak people. Peacemaking requires discernment, restraint, emotional maturity, humility, and Wisdom. Peacemaking requires soul prosperity. It requires the ability to recognize when conflict is necessary and when ego, fear, pride, insecurity, projection, or unresolved pain are inflaming situations unnecessarily.

David understood this with Saul. Saul became deeply hostile toward David, yet David repeatedly refused to destroy him prematurely even when opportunities appeared available. David discerned that vengeance was not his assignment. David did not touch the anointed of God.

Jesus taught love your enemy, not because enemies are always trustworthy, safe, or harmless, but because **hatred creates bondage**. Human beings can become permanently entangled with people they **hate**. A person can become soul tied with someone they hate. Some people remain emotionally chained to old battles for decades because they never stop rehearsing the conflict internally.

Some people remain blocked because they never stop fighting. You cannot walk freely while dragging every old battle behind you. This does not mean peace always requires proximity. Making Peace is not always trust, agreement, reunion, unrestricted access, vulnerability, or denial.

We are told to forgive 70 X 7, even daily, but that does not mean not to handle spiritual business spiritually. Do not misunderstand forgiveness; it is a power that should not be misused, abused, or left unused. Forgiveness does not mean pretending nothing happened, removing all boundaries, or reentering destructive situations without Wisdom—even if those folks are your relatives. Mature Peace understands distinctions. There can be forgiveness without foolishness. There can be boundaries without hatred. There can be discernment without paranoia. There can be Peace without proximity. There can be release without reconciliation. There can be prayer without access.

Some relationships should not be restored to former intimacy simply because forgiveness occurred. Wisdom still matters. Safety still matters. Discernment still matters. God does not require people to abandon Wisdom or risk their life in order to prove they are loving.

Do not become so accustomed to conflict that Peace feels uncomfortable.

Spiritual maturity is not reacting emotionally to every situation. It is learning obedience, restraint, Wisdom, and timing.

After an entire book about blockers, warfare, systems, entanglement, obstruction, movement, and strategy, the mature ending is freedom in Christ. The Lord never intended you to be blocked from the assignments, purposes, gains and lands He has prepared for you. If blockers arise, learn to discern and see them clearly. Sometimes learning to move, remove or navigate around them is the entire purpose and the lesson so that what the Lord has given to you can be attained and also kept and maintained by you. We are not the scorched Earth crowd, we do not war against flesh and blood; we do things God's way, decently and in order.

Only if the Lord says so. If the Lord says to walk away, do that. If He says stand and fight spiritually and legally, then do that. If He says to keep them in prayer, then do that. If He says stop praying for them, then you do that.

AMEN.

Dear Reader

Thank you for acquiring this book and supporting this ministry. I pray this book has accomplished what it set out to do--, help you recognize and break every ungodly soul tie.

Shalom,

Dr. Marlene Miles

I seal these words, decrees, declarations and prayers herein across every realm, age, era, dimension, and timeline, past present and future and to infinity. I seal them with the Blood of Jesus and the Holy Spirit of Promise.

Let every retaliation against this speaker, the listener, backfire without Mercy, to infinity against the evil perpetrator, in the Name of Jesus. **Amen.**

New Releases:

Christ of God (*The*) 3-book series

Christ of God, (*The*) Box Set, includes all 3 books

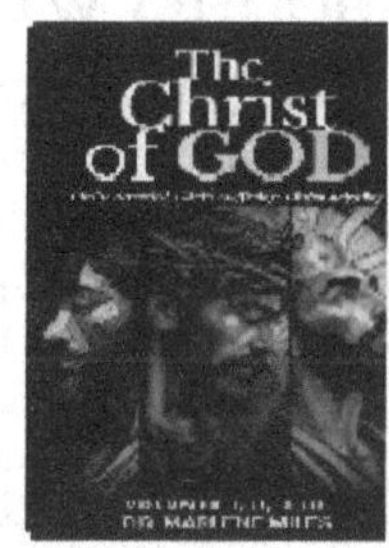

Prayerbooks by this author

There are some books that are only prayers. You just open up the book and pray.

FAKE FRIENDS: *Prayers Against Betrayers*

HOLIDAY WARFARE Prayer Manual (humorous) Surviving Family Gatherings All Year Long (without catching a case)

SOUL TIE Prayer Manual (The) Part of a 3-part series including a workbook.

MAD at DADDY Prayer Manual – part of a 3-part series including a workbook.

Healing the Sibling & Relative Wound Prayer Manual

Healing the Father-Son Wound Prayer Manual

Prayers Against Barrenness: *For Success in Business and Life*

Breaking Curses of the Mother Prayer Manual

Prayers Against Barrenness: *For Success in Business and Life*

Fruit of the Womb: *Prayers Against Barrenness*

Beauty Curses, *Warfare Prayers Against*
https://a.co/d/5Xlc2OM

Courts of Marriage: Prayers for Marriage in the Courts of Heaven *(prayerbook)* https://a.co/d/cNAdgAq

Courtroom Warfare @ Midnight *(prayerbook)*
https://a.co/d/5fc7Qdp

Demonic Cobwebs *(prayerbook)* https://a.co/d/fp9Oa2H

Every Evil Bird https://a.co/d/hF1kh1O

Gates of Thanksgiving

Spirits of Death, Hell & the Grave, Pass Over Me and My House

Throne of Grace: Courtroom Prayer

Warfare Prayer Against Poverty https://a.co/d/bZ61lYu

Other books by this author

Abundance of Jesus (The) https://a.co/d/5gHJVed

AK: The Adventures of the Agape Kid

Already Married in the Spirit: *Why You May Not Be Married in the Natural*

AMONG SOME THIEVES https://a.co/d/dkYT4ZV

Ancestral Powers

Anti-Karen: *How To Mind Your Own Business Without Minding Other People's*

Anti-Marriage, *The Spirit of*

Backstabbers https://a.co/d/gi8iBxf

Barrenness, *Prayers Against* https://a.co/d/feUltIs

Battlefield of Marriage, *The*

Beware of the Dog: Prayers Against Dogs in the Dream.

Bless Your Food: *Let the Dining Table be Undefiled* *https://a.co/d/6oPMRDv*

Blindsided: *Has the Old Man Bewitched You?* https://a.co/d/5O2fLLR

Break Free from Collective Captivity

Broken Spirits & Dry Bones

By Means of a Whorish Father

Caged Life: Get Out Alive! https://a.co/d/bwPbksX

Casting Down Imaginations

Christ of God (*The*) 3-book series

Christ of God, (*The*) Box Set, includes all 3 books

Churchzilla, The Wanna-Be, Supposed-to-be Bride of Christ https://a.co/d/eAf5j3x

Collateral Damage: *When What Happened Spiritually Was Your Fault*

Deep Poverty: Get Out of Poverty and Its Shame

Demonic Cobwebs (prayerbook)

Demonic Time Bombs

Demons Hate Questions

Devil Loves Trauma, *The*

Devil Weapons: Unforgiveness, Bitterness,...

The Devourers: Thieves of Darkness 2

Do Not Swear by the Moon

Don't Refuse Me, Lord (4 book series)

https://a.co/d/idP34LG

Dream Defilement

The Emptiers: *Thieves of Darkness, 1*
https://a.co/d/5I4n5mc

Entanglements:

Evil Touch

Failed Assignment

Fantasy Spirit Spouse https://a.co/d/hW7oYbX

FAT Demons (The): *Breaking Demonic Curses*
https://a.co/d/4kP8wV1

Fear of Money (The)

The Fold (5-book series)

- The Fold (Book 1)
- Name Your Seed (Book 2)
- The Poor Attitudes of Money (3)
- Do Not Orphan Your Seed (4)
- For the Sake of the Gospel (5)
- My Sowing Journal

Gang Ups: Touch Not God's Anointed

Gathered: No Longer Scattered
https://a.co/d/1i5DPIX

Getting Rid of Evil Spiritual Food

https://a.co/d/i2L3WYQ

got HEALING? Verses for Life

got LOVE? Verses for Life https://a.co/d/8seXHPd

got HOPE? Verses for Life

got money? https://a.co/d/g2av41N

Has My Soul Been Sold? https://a.co/d/dyB8hhA

Here Come the Horns: *Skilled to Destroy* https://a.co/d/cZiNnkP

Hidden Sins: Hidden Iniquity

https://a.co/d/4Mth0wa

How to Dental Assist

How to Dental Assist2: Be Productive, Not Wasteful

How To Stay Prayed Up

How to STOP Being a Blind Witch or Warlock

I Take It Back

In Multiplying I Will Multiply Thee

Into Freedom:

Irresistible: Jesus' Triumphal Entry https://a.co/d/d09IfEC

KISS OF BAAL (*The*)

KNOW YOUR BATTLE: Stop Swinging Blindly — and Win Against Opponents, Adversaries & Enemies (Workbook) https://a.co/d/eOwFKlV

Legacy

Let Me Have A Dollar's Worth
https://a.co/d/h8F8XgE

Level the Playing Field

Living for the NOW of God https://a.co/d/6bK5duE

Lose My Location https://a.co/d/crD6mV9

Love Breaks Your Heart

Mad At Daddy: Healing Father-Wounds that Affect Motherhood (book, workbook & prayer manual)

Made Perfect In Love

Mammon https://a.co/d/29yhMG7

Man Safari, *The*

Marriage Ed.: *Rules of Engagement & Marriage*

Made Perfect in Love

Money Hunters: Beware of Those

Money on the Altar https://a.co/d/4EqJ2Nr

Mulberry Tree, *The* https://a.co/d/9nR9rRb

Motherboard (The)- *Soul Prosperity Series*

Name Your Seed

Occupy: *Until I Return* https://a.co/d/bZ7ztUy

One Defining Day*: A Day When Dreams Come True*

Opponent, Adversary, or Enemy?: Fight The Right Battle with the Right Weapons

https://a.co/d/byQqEE2 & companion workbook: Know Your Battle

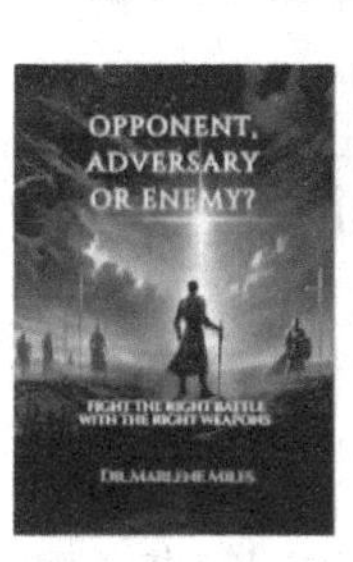

Plantation Souls

Players Gonna Play

Portals: Shut the Front Door: Prayers to Close Evil Portals.

Power Money: Nine Times the Tithe

https://a.co/d/gRt41gy

The Power to Get Wealth https://a.co/d/e4ub4Ov

Powers Above

Red Flags & Green Flags

The Robe, Part 1, The Lessons of Joseph

The Robe, Part II, The Lessons of Joseph

Seasons of Grief

Seasons of Siege: God Is Coming

Seasons of Waiting

Seasons of War

Second Marriage, Third--, *Any Marriage*

https://a.co/d/6m6GN4N

Seducing Spirits: Idolatry & Whoredoms

https://a.co/d/4Jq4WEs

Shut the Front Door: *Prayers to Close Portals*
https://a.co/d/cH4TWJj

Siege: *God Is Coming*

Sift You Like Wheat

Six Men Short: What Has Happened to all the Men?

SLAVE

Sleep Afflictions & Really Bad Dreams
https://a.co/d/f8sDmgv

Soul Prosperity soul prosperity series 3

https://a.co/d/5p8YvCN

Much more teaching on Soul Ties and getting free from them in the series: SOUL TIES: HOW THEY FORM AND HOW TO BREAK THEM (book, workbook, and prayer manual) **https://a.co/d/01jVIb0C https://a.co/d/09zdVVYe https://a.co/d/0dzaDiU3**

Soul Ties: How Soul Ties Form, and How To Break Them (book, workbook & prayer manual)

Soul Ties2: The Pull

Souls In Captivity

The Spirit of Anti-Marriage

The Spirit of Poverty https://a.co/d/abV2o2e

Spiritual Thieves https://a.co/d/eqPPz33

StarStruck- Triangular Power series.

SUNBLOCK- Triangular Power series.

The Swallowers: *Thieves of Darkness*, 3

Take It Back

This Is NOT That: How to Keep Demons from Coming at You

Time Is of the Essence

Too Many Wives: *Why You Have Lady Problems*

Tormenting Spirits https://a.co/d/dAogEJf

Toxic Souls

Triangular Power *(series),* Powers Above, SUNBLOCK, Do Not Swear by the Moon, TARSTRUCK

TRIBE: *What Covenants Are Governing You…?*

Unbreak My Heart: *Don't Let Me Die*

Uncontested Doom

Ungovered Hunger: How Unchecked Appetite Dismantles Authority

Unguarded Hours, *The*

Unseen Life, *The* (forthcoming)

Upgrade: How to Get Out of Survival Mode Toxic Souls (Book 2 of series) , Legacy (Book 3 of series)

The Wasters: *Thieves of Darkness,* Bk 2 https://a.co/d/bUvI9Jo

What Have You to Declare? What Do You Have With You from Where You've Been?

When I Was A Child, *I Prayed As a Child*

When the Devourer is Rebuked https://a.co/d/1HVv8oq

When The Table Is Set Against You

WTH? Get Me Out of This Hell https://a.co/d/a7WBGJh

The Wilderness Romance ***(series)*** This series is about conducting a Godly relationship and marriage with someone who is a Wilderness person. ***The Social Wilderness***

- ***The Sexual Wilderness***
- ***The Spiritual Wilderness***

Other Series

The Fold (a series on Godly finances)

https://a.co/d/4hz3unj

Soul Prosperity Series https://a.co/d/bz2M42q

Spirit Spouse books

https://a.co/d/9VehDSo

https://a.co/d/97sKOwm

Battlefield of Marriage, The https://a.co/d/eUDzizO

Players Gonna Play

https://a.co/d/2hzGw3N

Sent Spirit Spouse (can someone send you a spirit spouse? This book is not yet released.)

Thieves of Darkness series

The Emptiers https://a.co/d/heio0dO

The Wasters https://a.co/d/5TG1iNQ

The Swallowers https://a.co/d/1jWhM6G

The Devourers: Why We Can't Have Nice Things https://a.co/d/87Tejbf

Dr. Marlene Miles is a teacher, author, and spiritual thinker known for her grounded, discerning approach to prayer and spiritual formation. Her work emphasizes clarity, restraint, and maturity in faith—helping believers move beyond emotionalism and performance into a steady, practiced walk with God.

With a deep respect for Scripture and a practical understanding of daily life, Dr. Miles writes for those who want their prayer life to be formed, not dramatized. Her teaching encourages spiritual maintenance, discernment, and responsibility—so faith remains strong not only in crisis, but in everyday living.

www.ingramcontent.com/pod-product-compliance
Lightning Source LLC
LaVergne TN
LVHW030921080826
845145LV00013B/2998
9781971933719